nk you
very
uch
Love
ur
od from
izzy

I ♥ed your food
Alex

e food
Great

I really liked the food you made
Juan

Thank you
from Nick!!

you made Bobo Love Kyra

densy

thank you chef
Bob from Mijeah

claire

nk you for
ng for our
school this
Jakem

Pete
Matt
Thank You!

thank you
from Jimmy

you

Ryan!!!!!!!!!!!

Analeeq

Thank you,
Ben

Dear Bobo
thank you so
much for the
food It was
wonderful. The
food last year
was Yuky.

You did a geat Job at making our food this year good Job Benny

Thank You Chef Bobo from Carlo

Thank You for ~~from~~ The Dessert!!

P.S. And The food by Bella

you make the best chicken! from Carner

Thank you for The yummy!! food from ArDeN

Your cooking w this year Melanie

Chef John.

you make this School special Alex

Dear BoBo, ♡♡♡ I Love YouR food and Desserts and you. Love Lynnette P.s. and my family says Thank you

yum

Thank you from Taki

CHEF BOBO'S
GOOD FOOD
COOKBOOK

Meredith® Books
Des Moines, Iowa

Chef Bobo's Good Food Cookbook
by Robert W. Surles

Editor: Jan E. Miller
Contributing Writer: Stephanie Pearson
Senior Associate Design Director: Mick Schnepf
Assistant Art Director: Erin Burns
Contributing Editor: Linda Henry
Copy Chief: Terri Fredrickson
Publishing Operations Manager: Karen Schirm
Edit and Design Production Coordinator: Mary Lee Gavin
Book Production Managers: Pam Kvitne, Marjorie J. Schenkelberg, Rick von Holdt, Mark Weaver
Contributing Copy Editor: Maria Duryée
Contributing Proofreaders: Judith Friedman, Gretchen Kauffman, Donna Segal
Editorial Assistant: Cheryl Eckert
Food Photography: Robert Jacobs, Blaine Moats
Staff and Children Photography: Robert Jacobs, Susan B. Markisz
Food Stylists: Paige Boyle, Charles Worthington
Prop Stylist: Sue Mitchell
Indexer: Elizabeth Parson

Meredith® Books
Editor in Chief: Linda Raglan Cunningham
Design Director: Matt Strelecki
Managing Editor: Gregory H. Kayko
Executive Editor: Jennifer Dorland Darling

Publisher: James D. Blume
Executive Director, Marketing: Jeffrey Myers
Executive Director, New Business Development: Todd M. Davis
Executive Director, Sales: Ken Zagor
Director, Operations: George A. Susral
Director, Production: Douglas M. Johnston
Business Director: Jim Leonard

Vice President and General Manager: Douglas J. Guendel

Meredith Publishing Group
President: Jack Griffin
Senior Vice President: Bob Mate

Meredith Corporation
Chairman and Chief Executive Officer: William T. Kerr
President and Chief Operating Officer: Stephen M. Lacy

In Memoriam: E.T. Meredith III (1933-2003)

Chef Bobo?! "Is that your real name?"

Chef Bobo? I know the questions by heart: "Is that your real name?" "How did you get it?" Truth be told, my good friend Jodie Morrow bestowed the title, and I've been using the nickname since my career in food began. It's affectionate and it embodies my philosophy of being comfortable and having fun in the kitchen. Some of the kids at The Calhoun School have asked if it is my real name, and I always say, "Of course!" (although they know my real name is Robert Surles).

No matter which name I answer to, on any given school day you will find me and my talented team in The Calhoun School kitchen working hard. It's important work, but there is always laughter as we lovingly prepare meals for special people. That's what I do, and that is what this cookbook is all about: food, love, and fun. It is my opportunity to teach families the importance of sharing the pleasure of making and enjoying wonderful meals together.

I think of the kitchen in every home as a center of community, just as it is at Calhoun. The kitchen is a wonderful place to talk, share time, and experiences. Working as a family to put healthful meals on the table also teaches some fundamental life skills that should be developed as early as possible. It is only with those skills that the next generation will be able to reverse the increasing obesity rate and learn that homemade actually tastes better than fast food, junk food, and processed food.

So this book is my way of helping parents see it isn't difficult to make healthful, nourishing, joyful food a part of their children's future and their everyday family life. With those same skills, love, passion, and foolproof, kid-tested recipes, you'll want to spend more time in your kitchen having great family fun.

So enjoy and bon appetit!

Chef Bobo

Table of Contents

Dedication and Gratitude

This book is dedicated to the entire community of the Calhoun School, the students, the parents, the faculty and the administration. Their support and willingness to try new things make our work rewarding and fun every day. Also, the deepest gratitude to the best kitchen crew in the country, my Sous Chef, Melissa Rodriguez and Chefs Chris Canty, Tomek Koszylko and Ilya Malachias and Rosa Sandoval and Jose Roman. Everyday we have great fun creating absolutely amazing food with lots of love and laughter. I also have to thank my dear friends Lynne Calamia (my recipe tester) and Bob DiBenedetto for their support and encouragement. I will always be grateful to Chef Alain Sailhac, Dean and Executive Vice President of the French Culinary Institute, for remembering my dreams and for helping me to realize them. And to dear Stevie Pierson who took the words right out of my head.

Rosemary, Rutabaga Fries, and Life Lessons

> **"That's when I learned for sure that whether it was my grandma's Texas kitchen or a small Vietnamese open-air restaurant, the food that tasted best was authentic and fresh and prepared with care by a person I saw in the kitchen who loved what they were doing."**

Long before I was a chef and before I was called "Bobo," I started my love affair with food. I've been cooking since I was 7 years old. My mother died when I was 3, and my grandmother raised me and my two sisters while she worked full-time as an office clerk in downtown Dallas. When my grandma came home at the end of her long workday, no matter how tired she was, she would always prepare dinner for us. I loved being there to help her. "Mamo" wasn't a great cook, but the flavors in her food were honest, simple, and straightforward. We always had fun cooking together and we constantly laughed. Even though I could barely reach the top of the counter, she would let me peel, chop, stir, clean, and do just about anything else I wanted. She loved having help and I was thrilled to have the time to tell her about my day and to learn about cooking.

Those moments in the kitchen were always happy times. They taught me there is something magical about a kitchen filled with delicious aromas, laughter, and music. Washing dishes, drying them, putting away leftovers—it might have been routine to someone else. To me it was what family felt like. It was convivial and it was love.

So I've been cooking for my family and friends since. Food has always been an important part of my life, so at every stage of my life I set out to learn and experience as much about food and culture as I could—whether it was visiting friends and experiencing the flavors of the Deep South, exploring outrageous new flavors of the traditional dishes of New Orleans, or discovering the restaurants, recipes, cuisines, and flavors in New York. Yet, somehow it never occurred to me that food could be a profession.

I spent the bulk of my career in corporate life working for Air France in their human resources department for the U.S.A. That job literally and figuratively opened the world up for me. I was lucky enough to travel to some 60 countries where I sought out the food of working

families which I found to have the boldest flavors while being simplest to prepare. That's when I learned for sure that whether it was my grandma's kitchen or a small Vietnamese open-air restaurant, the food that tasted best was authentic, fresh, and prepared with care by people I saw in the kitchen who loved what they were doing.

Upon leaving Air France I decided I never wanted to wear a suit and tie again and now was the time to pursue my passions. What was it I loved more than anything in the world? What gave me immense pleasures? What had I been doing instinctively since I was a little kid? Hmmm....

Chapter 2

In June 2000, I enrolled in a six-month course at the famed French Culinary Institute in New York City to learn how to organize a professional kitchen and perfect my cooking techniques. I loved every minute of cooking school and this new world. I totally immersed myself in it. So much so that at once I was a caterer, a culinary student, a culinary graduate, and a cooking school teacher. Talk about making up for lost time!

In this newly charmed life, one thing led to another. A year and a half after working at The French Culinary Institute (FCI), Chef Alain Sailhac, dean and executive vice president of the FCI, called me to his office to talk about my "career." Alain is one of the world's leading chefs and a member of the James Beard House Hall of Fame. He knows so much about food and people. He knew of my dream to cook for children and teach them about good food. He remembered and recommended me for an opening at The Calhoun School, a friendly, progressive, nurturing private school in New York City for children from kindergarten to 12th grade. I not only took the job, I soon invited four of my top French Culinary Institute students to join me in Calhoun's kitchen.

Enter the Calhoun School

And that's where you'll find me and my staff today—and every day of the school year—feeding more than 500 students and staff for breakfast, lunch, and after-school programs. But it's not just about feeding kids. It's about health, nutrition, and well-being. It's about food as a life skill—teaching kids how to prepare food, how to cook meals, and how to eat them. Most of all, it's about love for the discovery and love for the process. These are the ingredients that my staff at The Calhoun School bring to work every day. To say these chefs are talented—and indeed they are—is important, but the spirit

"It's not just about feeding the kids. It's about health, nutrition, and well-being. It's about food as a life skill."

5

> **"I want kids to know what food really tastes like. My experience has taught me that children—even the youngest—will eat (and love) healthful food if it tastes good."**

with which they use their talents is what makes the Calhoun community understand my belief of just how profoundly you can impact someone's life with the food you offer them.

My Mission

My philosophy, goals, and the reason for this book all come down to three things: I want kids to know what food really tastes like. I believe the best way to make sure adults eat well is to help them develop an appetite for healthful foods when they are young. My experience has taught me that children—even the youngest—will eat (and love) healthful food if it tastes good.

Not the Ketchup

My mantra from day one was "fresh, flavorful, natural, balance, variety, and made from scratch." Because I wanted the kids to start really tasting the food, I banned the ketchup and took away the mayonnaise. "Why?" they asked me, shocked. "Because I don't believe in it," I told them. I took away the sweetened fruit drinks, the soft drinks, and most of the packaged snacks and sweets. I insisted that when they asked for a bagel that they eat a piece of fruit first. I only served a dessert other than fresh fruit once a week. I cut the portion sizes; ratcheted up the flavors; made sure there were always choices and alternatives; replaced fatty foods, such as french fries, with oven-roasted rutabaga fries; made salad dressings from scratch; had a nourishing hot soup option on the lunch menu every day; and swore to them that fish didn't have to be "yucky" or "gross." Then I set out to prove it.

My staff, with good humor and infinite patience, helped to gradually introduce kids to unfamiliar tastes and to persuade them to consider foods they would normally reject (anything green or with scales topped that list). I remember one of the best days of our first year working together. It was a day in late May when 8-year-old Jason said the words, "Oh, all right, I'll try it" to a piece of fish. After seven long months of unsuccessfully trying every known tactic—from singing the praises of the taste of the fish to flattering his excellent taste in food, from offering him a little sample to pointing out how much his friends liked it, and promising him seconds on the rice that went with it—there were discreet high fives all around.

Flavorful and Tactful Lead to Success

Rather shamelessly, my staff and I made sure from the beginning that the intoxicating smell of freshly baking bread wafted up every morning from the school kitchen to the classroom floors. Then every week or two, we took off our chef hats and put on our teaching hats. We went into the classrooms to show kids what an artichoke looks like before it's cooked. We offered them a taste of tomorrow's artichoke and lima bean stew, and discussed with them how and why the food traditions of a different country vary so greatly from our own. Demystifying food, romancing it, and putting it in the context of a different culture was eye-opening and fascinating to them. We started after-school cooking classes for second-, third- and fourth-graders and for the high school kids. We got rid of the old, stale salad bar and with the input of kids—some vegetarian— we turned it into a colorful global farmer's market, filled with everything from fresh heirloom beets to crunchy sprouts and silken tofu, to baby lettuces, pumpkin seeds, guacamole, and loads of fresh fruit.

A Man of Many Hats

At times, I admit, I feel less like a classically trained chef than some fantastic amalgam of chef, teacher, diplomat, salesman, negotiator, cheerleader, and child psychologist. One day when we had Parmesan chicken, macaroni and cheese, and Brussels sprouts (a notorious hard sell) for lunch, I had the following conversation in the lunch line with the lower school kids:

Adorable third-grader: "Chef Bobo, can I have some more chicken ?"
Me (in a slightly stern voice): "Do you know what the price of the chicken is?"
Adorable third-grader (looking confused): "No."
Me: "Three Brussels sprouts."
Adorable third-grader smiles broadly and takes three Brussels sprouts with the chicken.

By the end of lunch, I got a lot more Brussels sprouts into kids' mouths than they would have had without my negotiating and cajoling. I didn't care if they didn't like them upon first try—at least they tried them.

Sweet Rewards

Does it sound like a hard job? It is. But to work with kids is a joy. This has been the most wonderful experience of my life. And would the chef at a fancy three-star restaurant get love letters painstakingly written in Day-Glo crayon or get to hear a satisfied customer confide, "Don't tell my mom, but your miso soup is much better than hers." Frankly, there aren't too many restaurants I know where the diners stand on their chairs and clap for you.

"Frankly, there aren't too many restaurants I know where the diners stand up on their chairs and clap for you."

The real joy is that my philosophy is working. The results are astonishing and the changes have been profound, on every level. When I started, kids were eating one case of vegetables a day. Now we're up to five cases a day. Because their tastes have evolved and they eat so many fruits and vegetables, 90 percent of what I serve is vegetarian. Because the food is so delicious and boldly flavored, picky eaters are constantly reminded of how much fun it is to eat. Because the kids aren't just getting "kid food," even the most finicky eaters have opened their eyes and palates to a wealth of tastes and wonderful choices. They may not know how to pronounce quinoa or jicama, but they love it! Junk food junkies have been given a solid re-education in the difference between fast food and good food. The kids have more energy; their teachers say they are more attentive and productive. They aren't in sugar shock after lunch or ravenous when they get out of school at 3:00 p.m.

For me, it has been a very sweet triumph and the realization of a dream. I am serving kids simple food that is simply wonderful, food prepared with the most natural ingredient of all—love. I am also teaching a lesson in how it is possible to fight the insidious fast-food/junk food/processed food world kids live in today. "Cooking up a revolution, one rutabaga fry at a time," as Michelle Norris of National Public Radio put it after a visit to the Calhoun lunchroom.

Start Your Own Revolution!

What I'm doing at school, you can do at home. You don't need to be a great chef or even an experienced cook. Make your kitchen an inviting place to be, focus on wholesome food that tastes good, and don't expect your kids to rave about your kohlrabi or ask for seconds of the salmon the first time you serve it. It's pretty straightforward from there. Here's what works!

• **Skip the kid food. Add big bold flavors.**

The best food for kids isn't kid food. Of course, kids love pizza, pasta, french fries, and brownies. But given a chance, they also will love everything from broccoli sprouts to garbanzo beans. Not only do they not need to live on kid food, kids don't deserve bland, safe tastes. They don't need their food to be deep-fried, overly sweet, heavily salted, or drowned in sauce. And there's no reason to wait until you think your kids are more mature to try new flavors. Chef Ilya Malachias, who grew up in a New Orleans food family, says, "I think food is like language. If you pick it up early, it's just easier and more natural."

"Just skip the fast-food takeout, the microwave, convenience food, the frozen pizza."

• **Suprise them with new flavors, combinations, textures, and spices.** Don't be afraid to introduce your kids to unfamiliar flavors. Try Indian or Asian dishes. Sometimes the unfamiliar promotes a sense of adventure and intrigue for kids. It works because food is global and global food is fun—our kids love crunchy Vietnamese summer rolls, sizzling Chinese dumplings, and flavorful miso soup. Food is one way you can open up the world to your child.

• **Moderate Portion Sizes**

Even when serving wholesome, good-for-you food, you still need to be mindful of serving sizes. We're battling childhood obesity partially because of the expanding portion sizes in restaurants, prepackaged snack foods, and other convenience items. It's hard to say no to kids because you love them, but it's important to teach moderation when kids are young.

• **Getting Kids Involved Makes It Fun**

Haven't you noticed how people tend to gather in the kitchen? It's the heart of the home. Turn on the music, throw on the aprons, and get cooking with your kids! It works because kids like to be involved. Children love to make pizza from scratch, vinaigrettes for salads and to whisk things together. Teens love making more complicated recipes. The most fun we had this year in our high school cooking class was teaching chocolate soufflés—no one was absent that day! When kids are participating—whether they're in kindergarten or high school— growing their own herbs, picking fresh strawberries at the farmer's market or baking you a birthday cake, they'll appreciate the experience even more.

Some parents think that if kids are involved cooking will take longer. My answer is that it does take more time. But isn't it worth it? At the risk of sounding corny, what you're really doing is sharing with your child, passing family rituals to the next generation, educating them about what they put in their mouths, and turning the family kitchen into a welcoming respite from the world.

Of course, it's easy to list principles and give helpful tips. In an ideal world, you would hear your child say—and yes, there is a fifth-grader at Calhoun who actually said this: "Broccoli sprouts are my favorite food." But in your world, the

following is the dialogue you might hear instead. It's verbatim, by the way, compliments of Chef Tomek Koszylko.

Calhoun Lunch Line:

Chef Tomek: "Do you want any bok choy?"

Kid (looking suspiciously and making face): "None for me."

Chef Tomek: "Have you ever tasted it?"

Kid: "No, but I know it's gross."

We have observed in our daily lunch line that it might take 10 or 15 times of serving a new food for a child to actually try a taste. So have patience, then have some more. Don't give in to all of your child's whims or whines, but on the other hand, remember that it's not Nutrition Boot Camp. My mentor Chef Alain Sailhac says, "Chef Bobo knows how to push gently and nicely." That's what I would suggest you do too.

In an ideal world, you would cook every night—from scratch. In the real world, we're all busy and frazzled and overworked. My suggestion is cook up a vegetable stock (page 56) on the weekend so during the week you can throw in some broccoli or tomatoes, puree it, and have a welcoming dinner. Add some potatoes or pasta, and you're set. If you absolutely don't have time to cook, find a local take-out place that makes their own roast chicken or a homemade minestrone. Just skip the fast food, the microwave convenience food, and the frozen pizza.

Bobo's No List:

• Processed food.

• **Junk food.** Of course, allow the occasional potato chip, but at least make it a baked potato chip.

• **Fast food.** Kids usually want to go to the closest drive-thru for the toy, not the food. Maybe it's diabolical, but one of the best ways to get kids to see how truly awful fast food is, is to let it get cold and then examine it like a science experiment—get up close and personal with those fatty globules.

• Soda. Regular sodas contain a lot of simple sugar which means a lot of empty calories.

• Store-bought cookies. Purchased baked goods are full of hidden starches, preservatives, and fats.

• Ketchup. Hide the ketchup—at least until kids know how the food tastes without it.

• **"Lite" products.** They're a trap and not "lite" in fat or calories.

• Store-bought salad dressing. If purchasing salad dressings, choose one that is low in fat, sugar, and salt.

• The new "semi-homemade" philosophy of cooking. By adding something like a can of soup or an instant mix to a dish, you are adding unnecessary sodium, artificial ingredients and/or unhealthy fats.

• The word "No." Eating shouldn't be about deprivation and what I call "The World of No." You can have nutritional food that's satisfying.

When you do have time to cook, you'll find that all the recipes in this book are simple and straightforward. To me, simple doesn't mean boring. It can be creative and profoundly satisfying. You don't need exotic, hard-to-find ingredients. You won't find long lists of instructions. There are a lot of basic principles. Once you understand how to make a vinaigrette or how to roast vegetables, you won't need to follow a recipe. And this note of reassurance from Chef Melissa Rodriguez: "What I've learned about cooking—whether it's here at school or at home—is that everyone makes one bad oatmeal or one inedible fish fillet. When it comes to cooking, no one is perfect. But great things come out of mistakes and everyone shines in their own way."

So shine on!

> "What you're really doing is sharing with your child, passing family rituals to the next generation."

A few tips to make it work:

- **Be vigilant.** Read labels. Canned vegetables are usually high in sodium; packaged baked goods are filled with saturated fatty acids.

- **Keep fresh fruit and vegetables in your house at all times.** Don't buy cookies, candy, or processed snack foods to have on hand.

- **Get involved in your child's school.** Find out what's being served in the cafeteria and work to be an advocate for change.

- **Be a role model.** No matter what age your child is, he or she is more likely to eat something when he or she sees you eat it. More often than not, kids like what their parents like. You are (although it's not always easy to tell!) a powerful role model and you set the example. What you don't eat also matters.

- **Enjoy the process.** If you're enthusiastic about what you're serving for dinner, your kids may have a more open mind. I honestly believe anything made with love tastes better.

II

fresh **herbs** for fresh **flavor**

The secret to fresh flavor is fresh herbs. End of story. The real taste of any dish comes shining through when the right herb brings out all the flavor, whether it's a pinch of robust rosemary or a few sprigs of tangy mint.

Herb Appreciation

The scene: Calhoun cooking class. Second-graders were being introduced to fresh dill by one of the chefs. The kids were asked to examine, smell, and taste this mysterious green.

Chef: "What does dill make you think of?"

1st child: "A leaf?"

2nd child: "Hmmm....maybe grass. Or some kind of weed."

3rd child: "A kind of leaf."

4th child: "Gravlax."

Some kids know a lot about herbs! Most know almost nothing. If you want to educate your kids' palate (and show them the world that exists outside of chicken nuggets and pizza), teach them about the flavor of fresh herbs. That's how I start off the younger kids.

At the beginning of the school year, I teach them about the six most common herbs. They are the easiest to understand and use in cooking. We talk about the following herbs:

Parsley • Thyme • **Basil** • Rosemary • Oregano • Dill

Experiment first with the basic list above, and once kids get used to having herbs in their food, they will not only eat them without much fuss, they will be curious about new herbs. As your kids express interest in new flavors, branch out a little bit.

Some herbs are an acquired taste—such as tarragon and cilantro. Thanks to the popularity of salsa and chips, most kids have tasted cilantro.

Some herbs, like lemongrass, don't even look like herbs. Because we use lemongrass in soups and fish recipes, we take the lemongrass to the kids in their classrooms so they can learn about it before tasting. The kids usually ask, "What is this? It looks like wood." Once they see how to prepare it and discover what it tastes like, it's a lot less mysterious.

Chives

Basil

Rosemary

int Tea Syrup

Think of this refreshing syrup as a mint julep to sweeten your iced tea—that's how good it is. At Calhoun we make regular iced tea but brew this simple syrup to add to the tea. We put the syrup in a squeeze bottle to keep the younger kids from drinking it!

1 cup sugar

1 cup water

1 bunch fresh mint

1 1-inch piece fresh ginger, peeled and sliced

1. Bring the sugar, water, mint, and ginger to a boil. Remove from heat. Let the mixture steep for 30 minutes.

2. Strain the syrup, discarding the mint leaves and ginger. Transfer the syrup to a squeeze bottle and chill.

Makes: about 8 cups

Dill and Yogurt

The magic of just two ingredients! This dip is a perfect after-school snack. Kids happily dig in with crunchy raw vegetables or even pretzels.

1   cup plain low-fat yogurt

2   tablespoons chopped fresh dill

½   teaspoon salt

    Freshly ground black pepper

    Assorted raw vegetables

1. In a bowl combine yogurt, dill, and salt. Season to taste with pepper. Store in the refrigerator about 1 hour for the flavors to develop. Serve with assorted raw vegetables.

Makes: about 1 cup

Nutrition Facts per tablespoon: 10 cal., 0 g total fat (0 g sat. fat),
1 mg chol., 83 mg sodium, 1 g carbo., 0 g fiber, 1 g pro.
Daily Values: 3% calcium

Basil Pesto Sauce

I'm surprised how much kids love pesto. I think it's because basil is such an appealing herb. This fresh, green sauce is a natural on pasta, wonderful with shrimp or chicken, and a delicious way to brighten a vegetable soup.

2½ **cups fresh basil leaves**

¾ **cup extra-virgin olive oil or canola oil**

1 **teaspoon salt**

2 **cloves garlic, halved**

½ **cup grated Parmesan cheese**

¼ **cup grated Romano cheese**

½ **teaspoon grated lemon zest**

1. In a blender or food processor combine the basil leaves, olive oil, salt, and garlic. Blend or process until pureed. Pour into a bowl and whisk in the Parmesan cheese, Romano cheese, and lemon zest.

2. If preparing this for pasta, add a cup of pasta water that has been saved just before draining the pasta. Then mix the pesto sauce with the pasta and enjoy!

Note: Most pesto recipes call for pine nuts or walnuts. At Calhoun, we don't use any type of nuts to protect any student who may have a nut allergy, but you can easily add a couple of tablespoons of nuts if you like.

Makes: about 1½ cups
Nutrition Facts per 1 tablespoon: 73 cal., 8 g total fat (2 g sat. fat),
3 mg chol., 66 mg sodium, 1 g carbo., 1 g fiber, 2 g pro.
Daily Values: 4% vit. A, 2% vit. C, 4% calcium, 1% iron

For pesto, fresh herbs are a must. For most recipes I choose fresh instead of dry herbs. A hint: you can rarely put too much fresh herb in a dish. But if you're using dry, it's easy to go overboard, so take it easier with these.

Cilantro, Tomato, Cucumber, and Yogurt Raita

Bursting with bold flavor, this refreshing Indian dish is the best way I know to introduce kids to the harmonious zing of cumin and cilantro. Serve it as a dip with raw vegetables or spoon the mixture inside a whole wheat tortilla to make a wrap.

2 cups plain low-fat yogurt

¼ seedless cucumber, peeled and chopped into pieces the same size as the tomatoes

½ cup chopped tomato

¼ cup chopped fresh cilantro

I teaspoon salt

I teaspoon toasted cumin seeds

Freshly ground black pepper

I. Line a colander with a double thickness of cheesecloth or a white cotton napkin. Place colander in a bowl. Spoon yogurt into center of cloth. Let drain for at least I hour.

2. Meanwhile, combine cucumber, tomato, cilantro, salt, and cumin seeds.

3. Once the yogurt has finished draining, put it in a bowl and stir in the cucumber mixture. (Discard the water that has drained from the yogurt.) Season to taste with pepper. Let stand about 30 minutes before serving. Refrigerate raita in an airtight container for 3 to 4 days.

Makes: about I½ cups
Nutrition Facts per 2 tablespoons: 32 cal., I g total fat (0 g sat. fat), 2 mg chol., 225 mg sodium, 4 g carbo., 0 g fiber, 2 g pro.
Daily Values: 5% vit. A, 7% vit. C, 8% calcium, 2% iron

# Chives and Cream Cheese Spread

Top a toasted bagel, fill a sandwich, or eat this creamy spread melted and bubbly on grilled tomato slices. All three options make a perfect "first" for a kid encounter with chives.

1 **8-ounce package reduced-fat cream cheese (Neufchâtel), softened**

2 **tablespoons chopped fresh chives**

3 **drops hot pepper sauce**

1. In a mixing bowl beat cream cheese with a hand mixer until it becomes light and fluffy. Add the chives and the hot pepper sauce. Beat on low speed until combined.

Makes: about 1 cup

Nutrition Facts per 1 tablespoon: 37 cal., 3 g total fat (2 g sat. fat),
11 mg chol., 57 mg sodium, 0 g carbo., 0 g fiber, 1 g pro.
Daily Values: 4% vit. A, 1% calcium

Tomato, Garlic, and Oregano Crostini

Kids think of oregano as the "pizza herb." So it isn't surprising kids delight in these crostini—it's like eating little pizzas. The recipe is both a guaranteed hit and a soon-to-be staple in your cooking repertoire! Serve them as a snack, a party hors d'oeuvre, or with a bowl of soup for lunch.

1 loaf unsliced crusty Italian bread or baguette-style French bread, cut diagonally into ½-inch-thick slices

¼ cup olive oil or olive oil-flavored nonstick cooking spray

Salt

Freshly ground black pepper

2 Beefsteak tomatoes, halved

1 clove garlic, smashed

½ cup chopped fresh oregano

Chopped Beefsteak tomato (optional)

1. Preheat oven to 350°F. Line a baking sheet with parchment paper or foil.

2. Arrange bread on the prepared baking sheet. Lightly brush bread with a little olive oil or spray with cooking spray. Lightly sprinkle a little salt and pepper over bread.

3. Bake, turning once, until crisp and lightly browned, 8 to 10 minutes. Remove from oven and let cool. Rub each piece of toasted bread with garlic, then rub with the cut side of a tomato. Sprinkle with oregano and chopped tomato, if you like.

Makes: 18 crostini

Nutrition Facts per crostini: 46 cal., 3 g total fat (0 g sat. fat), 0 mg chol., 61 mg sodium, 5 g carbo., 0 g fiber, 1 g pro.
Daily Values: 1% vit. C, 1% calcium, 2% iron

One of the best ways to teach younger children about herbs and fresh flavor is to let them grow their own herbs at home. Keeping a simple pot of fresh rosemary on the windowsill teaches them about taking responsibility, allows them to see how something grows, and illustrates how easy it is to season food. They love to proudly announce: "It came from my own garden!"

# **R**osemary, Lemon Juice, and Garlic Marinade

This punchy, zesty Italian-inspired marinade takes virtually no time to prepare—it's easily started the night before. Use it to enliven everything from chicken, pork, or lamb to a firm fish like cod or monkfish. The little kids at Calhoun think it smells like a Christmas tree!

1	cup olive oil
½	cup chopped fresh rosemary
2	tablespoons fresh lemon juice
1	teaspoon lemon zest
1	teaspoon salt
1	clove garlic, halved
	Freshly ground black pepper

1. In a blender container combine oil, rosemary, lemon juice, lemon zest, salt, and garlic. Blend until combined. Season to taste with pepper.

2. Marinate meat, chicken, or fish in the refrigerator for 3 to 4 hours or overnight. Cook meat, chicken, or fish as desired.

Makes: about 1 cup

 *arragon Tartar Sauce*

When we serve fish, the kids prefer this tartar sauce to ketchup. The natural sweetness of the tarragon, the saltiness of capers, the punch of the cornichon, the lemony tang…yum. No wonder we always run out!

- 1 **cup mayonnaise**
- ¼ **cup chopped cornichons***
- 1 **tablespoon undrained capers**
- 1 **tablespoon finely chopped fresh tarragon**
- 1 **teaspoon fresh lemon juice**
- 1 **teaspoon finely chopped shallot**
- 1 **clove garlic, minced**

1. In a bowl combine mayonnaise, cornichons, capers, tarragon, lemon juice, shallot, and garlic. Cover and refrigerate at least 2 hours. Taste the sauce and if it needs more of anything, add it. If you like it more tart—add more lemon. If you like it more herbal—add more tarragon!

Makes: about 1½ cups

***Note:** Cornichons are pickles made from gherkin cucumbers.

Nutrition Facts per 1 tablespoon: 69 cal., 7 g total fat (1 g sat. fat),
5 mg chol., 84 mg sodium, 1 g carbo., 0 g fiber, 0 g pro.

25

salads

a refresher course

28

The crunch factor is a big deal with kids, but if a salad lacks flavor it's just another crunchy, boring salad. Add zip and zing to everyday salads with zesty vinaigrettes and surprising ingredients.

asic Vinaigrette

This works with just about any salad, and as you'll see from the following recipes, there are endless ways to vary it. Two helpful tips: the proportions for any vinaigrette are roughly 3 parts oil to one part acid. Remember that the key to getting a vinaigrette to emulsify is the mustard. Start the recipe ahead and let it sit for an hour or so before you add the olive oil.

⅓ cup white or red wine vinegar

1 teaspoon finely chopped shallot

1 teaspoon Dijon mustard

½ teaspoon salt

Black pepper

⅔ cup olive oil

1. In a blender combine vinegar, shallot, Dijon mustard, salt, and pepper. Pulse a few times to mix the ingredients together. Let stand for a few minutes so that flavors will develop.

2. With the blender set to low and the lid on, start the blender. Remove the plug in the lid and very slowly add the olive oil in a fine stream. The mustard will cause the vinegar and oil to emulsify, and the vinaigrette will thicken.

3. Turn off the blender and let thicken. Adjust seasonings to taste.

Makes: 1 cup
Nutrition Facts per 2 tablespoons: 165 cal., 18 g total fat (2 g sat. fat),
0 mg chol., 160 mg sodium, 1 g carbo., 0 g fiber, 0 g pro.
Daily Values: 1% iron

 rench Vinaigrette

In my opinion, the addition of tarragon gives this a slightly more sophisticated taste. Add more or less tarragon to suit your preference. The kids at school like it with just a hint of the herb. If you're making this in the blender, don't bother chopping the tarragon.

⅓ cup sherry vinegar

1 teaspoon finely chopped shallot

1 teaspoon Dijon mustard

1 teaspoon chopped fresh tarragon

½ teaspoon salt

Black pepper

1 clove garlic

⅔ cup extra-virgin olive oil or canola oil

1. In a blender combine vinegar, shallot, Dijon mustard, tarragon, salt, pepper, and garlic. Pulse a few times to mix the ingredients together. Let stand for a few minutes so that flavors will develop.

2. With the blender set to low and the lid on, start the blender. Remove the plug in the lid and very slowly add the olive oil in a fine stream. The mustard will cause the vinegar and oil to emulsify, and the vinaigrette will thicken.

3. Turn off the blender and let thicken. Adjust seasonings to taste.

Makes: about 1 cup
Nutrition Facts per tablespoon: 83 cal., 9 g total fat (1g sat. fat),
0 mg chol., 80 mg sodium, 0 g carbo., 0 g fiber, 0 g pro.

Asian Flavors Vinaigrette

The sesame and ginger imbue this vinaigrette with big Asian flavor. It's just the one to turn to when you're serving an Asian dinner, like Sweet-and-Sour Pork (page 116).

½ cup sherry vinegar

¼ cup chopped fresh cilantro

¼ cup soy sauce

1 tablespoon Dijon mustard

1 teaspoon grated fresh ginger

1 clove garlic

1 cup canola oil

1 tablespoon toasted sesame oil

¼ cup fresh lime juice

1 tablespoon toasted sesame seeds

Salt and black pepper

1. In a blender combine the vinegar, cilantro, soy sauce, Dijon mustard, ginger, and garlic. Pulse a few times to mix the ingredients together. Let stand for a few minutes so that flavors will develop.

2. Combine the canola oil and sesame oil in a measuring cup. With the blender set to low and the lid on, start the blender. Remove the plug in the lid and very slowly add the oil mixture in a fine stream. The mustard will cause the vinegar and oil to emulsify, and the vinaigrette will thicken.

3. Pour the vinaigrette into a bowl and whisk in the lime juice and sesame seeds. Season to taste with salt and pepper.

Makes: 2 cups
Nutrition Facts per tablespoon: 70 cal., 8 g total fat (1 g sat. fat),
0 mg chol., 145 mg sodium, 1 g carbo., 0 g fiber, 1 g pro.
Daily Values: 1% vit. A, 2% vit. C, 1% iron

Roasted Garlic Vinaigrette

Wake up just about any salad with this vinaigrette. The garlic gains a mellow sweetness from a simple combination of sauteing and roasting. One word of advice: Don't let the garlic get too dark while sautéing on the top of the stove.

1	tablespoon vegetable oil
6	cloves garlic
⅓	cup red wine vinegar
1	teaspoon finely chopped shallot
1	teaspoon Dijon mustard
½	teaspoon chopped fresh thyme
½	teaspoon salt
	Black pepper
⅔	cup olive oil

1. Preheat oven to 350°F.

2. Place a small ovenproof skillet over medium heat and add the 1 tablespoon vegetable oil. When the oil becomes hot, carefully add the garlic cloves, 1 at a time. Stir the cloves until they just begin to turn brown. At this point, transfer the skillet to the oven to finish roasting the garlic. Roast until the garlic is golden brown, 5 to 10 minutes. Remove skillet from oven and let garlic cool.

3. In a blender combine the roasted garlic cloves, vinegar, shallot, Dijon mustard, thyme, salt, and pepper. Pulse a few times to mix the ingredients together. Let stand for a few minutes so that flavors will develop.

4. With the blender set to low and the lid on, start the blender. Remove the plug in the lid and very slowly add the olive oil in a fine stream. The mustard will cause the vinegar and oil to emulsify, and the vinaigrette will thicken.

5. Turn off the blender and let thicken. Adjust seasonings to taste.

Makes: 1¼ cups
Nutrition Facts per tablespoon: 72 cal., 8 g total fat (1 g sat. fat),
0 mg chol., 64 mg sodium, 1 g carbo., 0 g fiber, 0 g pro.
Daily Values: 1% vit. C, 1% iron

Salad Secrets

The secret of a good salad is knowing a basic vinaigrette recipe. It's so simple!
All it takes to whisk together a good vinaigrette is three ingredients—oil, vinegar,
and mustard—and three minutes. A little tip: If you want your vinaigrette to be
zesty and creamy, don't add cream—add a little Dijon mustard.

Roasted Tomato Vinaigrette

Tomato lovers, rejoice! The essence of tomatoes infuses this mellow vinaigrette. It's sensational drizzled on top of ripe summer tomatoes. If you can find heirloom tomatoes, you'll be in heaven.

3   plum tomatoes

   Olive oil

1   teaspoon finely chopped shallot

1   recipe Basic Vinaigrette (made with red wine vinegar; see page 28)

1   teaspoon chopped fresh tarragon or ½ teaspoon dried tarragon, crushed

1   teaspoon chopped fresh basil or ½ teaspoon dried basil, crushed

1   clove garlic

1   teaspoon fresh lemon juice

1   teaspoon fresh lime juice

   Salt and black pepper

1. Preheat oven to 350°F.

2. Cut tomatoes in half and remove seeds. Brush with a little bit of olive oil and sprinkle with the shallots. Arrange tomato halves in a single layer on a baking sheet that has been lined with parchment paper or has been lightly oiled. Roast in oven until tomatoes begin to turn brown, about 10 minutes. Remove from oven and let cool.

3. In a blender combine roasted tomatoes, Basic Vinaigrette, tarragon, basil, and garlic. Pulse a few times to mix the ingredients together. Let stand for a few minutes so that flavors will develop. Pour vinaigrette into a bowl and whisk in lemon juice and lime juice. Adjust seasonings to taste with salt and pepper.

Makes: 1½ cups

Nutrition Facts per 2 tablespoons: 69 cal., 7 g total fat (1 g sat. fat),
0 mg chol., 53 mg sodium, 1 g carbo., 0 g fiber, 0 g pro.
Daily Values: 2% vit. A, 4% vit. C, 1% iron

ixed Green Salad with Creamy Italian Dressing

Just greens and just terrific! Toss together what you like, what's fresh, and what's seasonal. The only green to avoid is iceberg lettuce—it won't stand up to the other flavors. I don't recommend using packaged greens. I know others feel differently, but I am always concerned about their freshness.

3   cups torn assorted greens*

1   cup torn arugula

   Creamy Italian Dressing or any of the salad dressings or vinaigrettes in this book (see pages 28 to 33)

1. Combine the assorted greens and arugula in a bowl and cover with damp towels. Store in the refrigerator until ready to use.

2. Pour salad dressing or vinaigrette over the salad and toss. Serve immediately.

*Note: Choose romaine lettuce, red leaf lettuce, Bibb lettuce, spinach, or a combination of any greens you like in a salad.

Makes: 4 servings
Nutrition Facts per serving : 67 cal., 7 g total fat (1 g sat. fat),
0 mg chol., 65 mg sodium, 1 g carbo., 1 g fiber, 0 g pro.
Daily Values: 5% vit. A, 2% vit. C, 2% calcium, 2% iron

Creamy Italian Dressing:
1. In a blender combine $\frac{1}{3}$ cup red wine vinegar, 1 tablespoon chopped oregano, 2 teaspoons Dijon mustard, 1 teaspoon finely chopped shallots, 1 teaspoon fat-free sour cream, $\frac{1}{2}$ teaspoon chopped fresh thyme, $\frac{1}{2}$ teaspoon salt, black pepper, and 2 cloves garlic. Pulse a few times to mix the ingredients together. Let stand for a few minutes so that flavors will develop.

2. With the blender set to low and the lid on, start the blender. Remove the plug in the lid and very slowly add $\frac{2}{3}$ cup olive oil in a fine stream. The mustard will cause the vinegar and oil to emulsify, and the dressing will thicken.

3. Turn off the blender and allow to thicken. Adjust the seasonings to taste.

Makes: 1¼ cups
Nutrition Facts per tablespoon: 65 cal., 7 g total fat (1 g sat. fat),
0 mg chol., 70 mg sodium, 0 g carbo., 0 g fiber, 0 g pro.
Daily Values: 1% vit. C, 1% iron

Instead of prepackaged greens, buy fresh greens and wash them, then wrap them in paper towels. They'll keep in your crisper for a week so you can easily enjoy a fresh salad every night.

Spinach Salad with Honey-Mustard Vinaigrette

Want to get your kids to eat spinach? It's almost impossible not to like this fresh, sparkling salad tossed with a sweet, tangy dressing. There's little fat and no bacon at all—yet there's still lots of salty crunch.

1 pound fresh spinach

4 hard-boiled eggs

½ cup chopped walnuts (optional)

½ red onion, thinly sliced

½ cup pitted kalamata olives, halved

½ cup grated Parmesan cheese

Honey-Mustard Vinaigrette

1. Prepare the spinach by separating all the leaves. Fill a sink with cold water and place the leaves in the water. Spinach can be very sandy, so it needs to be immersed in water. Swirl the leaves around a few times and transfer to a colander. Let the water out of the sink and wash the grit from the bottom. Once again fill the sink with cold water. Take each spinach leaf, remove the tough stem, and return it to the water. When all the spinach is back in the water, swirl it again and transfer to the colander.

2. Dry the spinach leaves and tear them into bite-size pieces. Place in a bowl and cover with damp towels. Store in refrigerator until ready to use.

3. Divide the spinach among 4 salad plates or bowls. Rub 1 egg through a grater over each plate of spinach. Divide walnuts, onion, and olives among the salad plates, then sprinkle with Parmesan cheese. Drizzle each salad with Honey-Mustard Salad Dressing. Serve immediately.

Makes: 4 servings
Nutrition Facts per 1 serving with Honey Mustard Vinaigrette Dressing: 133 cal.,
6 g total fat (1 g sat. fat), 0 mg chol., 103 mg sodium, 21 g carbo., 2 g fiber, 1 g pro.
Daily Values: 110% vit. A, 5% vit. C, 2% calcium, 3% iron

Honey-Mustard Vinaigrette:

1. In a blender combine ⅓ cup white wine vinegar, ¼ cup honey, 2 tablespoons Dijon mustard, 1 teaspoon finely chopped shallot, 1 teaspoon chopped fresh tarragon, ½ teaspoon salt, black pepper, and 1 clove garlic. Pulse a few times to mix the ingredients together. Let stand for a few minutes so that flavors will develop.

2. With the blender set to low and the lid on, start the blender. Remove the plug in the lid and very slowly add ⅔ cup olive oil in a fine stream. The mustard will cause the vinegar and oil to emulsify, and the vinaigrette will thicken. Turn the blender off and let thicken. Adjust seasonings to taste.

Makes: 1¼ cups
Nutrition Facts per tablespoon: 80 cal., 7 g total fat (1 g sat. fat),
0 mg chol., 93 mg sodium, 4 g carbo., 0 g fiber, 0 g pro.
Daily Values: 1% iron

Honey-Mustard Vinaigrette
is a perfect balance of sweet, tart,
and creamy. It's a salad dressing,
a sandwich spread, a dipping sauce,
and a hands-down favorite with kids.

C aesar Salad

A simple toss of romaine, Parmesan, and croutons make up this classic Caesar. For a more garlicky taste, rub the bowl with fresh garlic. The healthiest and most flavorful part of the romaine (or any lettuce, for that matter) is the core. So don't throw it out when you're washing lettuce.

3 to 4 hearts romaine

¼ cup olive oil

2 cloves garlic

3 cups unseasoned croutons

Eggless Caesar Salad Dressing

1 lemon, juiced (about 4 teaspoons)

½ cup freshly grated Parmigiano-Reggiano cheese

Salt

Freshly ground black pepper

1. Prepare romaine by breaking all the leaves apart and washing under cold running water. Dry romaine and tear it into bite-size pieces. Place in a bowl and cover with damp towels. Store in the refrigerator until ready to use.

2. To make garlic croutons, heat the olive oil in a skillet over medium heat. When the oil is hot, add the garlic and turn the heat down to low. Cook and stir the garlic until it is golden brown. Remove garlic from skillet and discard, leaving the oil in the skillet. Turn the heat back to medium and add the croutons to the skillet. Cook and stir until golden brown. Drain on paper towels.

3. Pour some of the Eggless Caesar Salad Dressing over the romaine and toss. Sprinkle with lemon juice and cheese and toss again. Season to taste with salt and pepper. Finally, add the garlic croutons and toss. Serve immediately. Pass additional dressing, if you like.

Makes: 4 servings
Nutrition Facts per serving: 360 cal., 25 g total fat (8 g sat. fat),
24 mg chol., 794 mg sodium, 20 g carbo., 3 g fiber, 16 g pro.
Daily Values: 126% vit. A, 55% vit. C, 48% calcium, 12% iron

Eggless Caesar Salad Dressing:
1. In a blender combine ¾ cup extra-virgin olive oil or canola oil, 3 cloves garlic, and 1 teaspoon salt. Pulse a few times until garlic is pureed. Add ¼ cup white wine vinegar, 1 tablespoon Dijon mustard, and a dash of Worcestershire sauce to blender. With the blender set to low, cover and blend until combined.

Makes: 2 cups
Nutrition Facts per tablespoon: 94 cal., 10 g total fat (1 g sat. fat),
0 mg chol., 179 mg sodium, 0 g carbo., 0 g fiber, 0 g pro.
Daily Values: 1% iron

Even without eggs, a wholesome update of the traditional Caesar dressing comes surprisingly close to the original taste.

Arugula, Endive, Red Onion, Pears, and Walnut Salad

This may be my favorite salad of all. It's just bursting with flavor and every bite is a treat. What an all-star lineup! Ripe pear, crisp walnuts, fresh greens, sweet onion, all in a rich balsamic dressing.

1 bunch arugula

1 Belgian endive

1 ripe pear

½ small red onion, thinly sliced

½ cup walnuts, broken (optional)

Balsamic Vinaigrette

1. Prepare the arugula by washing it thoroughly in a sink or a deep container of cold water. Arugula is very sandy and must be cleaned by dunking in and out of the water. Change the water, pouring off all the sand, and refill the sink or container with fresh cold water. This should be done 3 times. Dry the arugula and tear into bite-size pieces. Place arugula in a bowl.

2. Separate the endive leaves from the core; wash, dry, and add them to the bowl with the arugula.

3. Cut the pear in half lengthwise. Remove the seeds, core, and stem. Thinly slice the pear. Add the pear and onion to the bowl with the arugula and endive. Sprinkle the walnuts over the salad. Toss the salad together.

4. Pour some of the Balsamic Vinaigrette over salad and toss. Serve immediately. If you like, pass remaining vinaigrette.

Makes: 4 servings
Nutrition Facts per serving with Balsamic Vinaigrette Dressing: 105 cal.,
7 g total fat (1 g sat. fat), 0 mg chol., 73 mg sodium, 11 g carbo., 3 g fiber, 1 g pro.
Daily Values: 21% vit. A, 11% vit. C, 4% calcium, 4% iron

Balsamic Vinaigrette:
1. In a blender combine ⅓ cup balsamic vinegar, 1 teaspoon finely chopped shallot, 1 teaspoon Dijon mustard, 1 teaspoon honey, ½ teaspoon salt, black pepper, and 1 clove garlic. Pulse a few times to mix the ingredients together. Let stand for a few minutes so that flavors will develop.

2. With the blender set to low and the lid on, start the blender. Remove the plug in the lid and very slowly add ⅔ cup olive oil in a fine stream. The mustard will cause the vinegar and oil to emulsify, and the vinaigrette will thicken. Turn the blender off and let thicken. Adjust seasonings to taste.

Makes: 1 cup
Nutrition Facts per tablespoon: 89 cal., 9 g total fat (1 g sat. fat),
0 mg chol., 81 mg sodium, 2 g carbo., 0 g fiber, 0 g pro.
Daily Values: 1% iron

Balsamic vinaigrette is the same as a basic vinaigrette except the sweet, dark taste of balsamic vinegar adds a little more richness. Kids love the bold flavor of balsamic—we always serve it on the salad bar.

exican Salad with Tortilla Strips, Cilantro and Lime Juice Dressing

This crunchy, healthful, beautifully constructed salad can be lunch all by itself. The "crunch" factor is important—kids love anything with crunch, so the golden brown tortilla strips make this a winner.

3 plum tomatoes, finely chopped

½ small red onion, finely chopped

1 stalk celery, finely chopped

1 small carrot, shredded

½ seedless cucumber, finely chopped

2 fresh jalapeño chile peppers, seeded and finely chopped

½ cup Cilantro and Lime Juice Dressing

Salt and black pepper

3 flour or corn tortillas, cut into strips

Nonstick cooking spray

1 head iceberg lettuce

½ cup shredded part-skim mozzarella cheese

1. Preheat oven to 350°F.

2. Combine the tomatoes, onion, celery, carrot, cucumber, and jalapeño peppers. Pour the Cilantro and Lime Juice Salad Dressing over the vegetables and set aside to marinate. Season to taste with salt and pepper, if necessary.

3. Roll up each of the flour tortillas and slice crosswise, which will result in long thin strips. Spray the tortilla strips with cooking spray and spread out on a baking sheet. Bake until they begin to turn golden brown, about 5 minutes. Remove from oven and set aside to cool.

4. Cut the head of lettuce into quarters. Separate the lettuce leaves and wash and dry them. Make 4 stacks of lettuce leaves.

5. To serve, place 1 stack of lettuce leaves on each salad plate. Top each with some of the marinated vegetables. Sprinkle a little mozzarella cheese over the top and add a few of the toasted tortilla strips. Serve immediately.

Makes: 4 servings
Nutrition Facts per serving with Cilantro and Lime Juice Dressing: 275 cal., 18 g total fat
(4 g sat. fat), 8 mg chol., 406 mg sodium, 24 g carbo., 4 g fiber, 7 g pro.
Daily Values: 77% vit. A, 52% vit. C, 16% calcium, 11% iron

Cilantro and Lime Juice Dressing:

1. In a bowl whisk together ¼ cup chopped cilantro, ¼ cup lime juice, 1 tablespoon finely chopped shallot, 1 teaspoon sugar or honey, ¼ teaspoon crushed red pepper flakes (if desired), ¼ teaspoon ground cumin, and 1 clove garlic, smashed. Whisk in ½ cup olive oil in a slow stream. Let stand for 30 minutes. Remove the smashed garlic. Season to taste with salt and black pepper.

Makes: 1 cup
Nutrition Facts per tablespoon: 66 cal., 7 g total fat (1 g sat. fat),
0 mg chol., 38 mg sodium, 2 g carbo., 0 g fiber, 0 g pro.
Daily Values: 2% vit. A, 7% vit. C, 1% calcium, 1% iron

If you love the distinctive taste of cilantro, this tangy Latin American vinaigrette is for you. It's not only good on salads, it's also an inspired way to add zest to plain black beans.

Tricolor Salad

Italians, well-known for their sense of taste and design, have designed this very pretty, very satisfying salad. Using just three ingredients, it boasts a successful marriage of texture and flavor.

1 head radicchio

2 Belgian endives

1 bunch arugula

Red Wine Vinaigrette or French Vinaigrette (page 29)

Crumbled Roquefort cheese (optional)

1. Separate the leaves of the radicchio; wash, dry, and tear them into bite-size pieces. Place in a bowl. Separate the endive leaves from the core; wash, dry, and chop them into bite-size pieces; add to the bowl with the radicchio.

2. Prepare the arugula by washing it thoroughly in a sink or a deep container of cold water. Arugula is very sandy and must be cleaned by dunking in and out of the water. Change the water, pouring off all the sand, and refill the sink or container with fresh cold water. This should be done 3 times. Dry the arugula and tear into bite-sized pieces. Add to the bowl with the radicchio and endive.

3. Pour some of the Red Wine Vinaigrette or French Vinaigrette over salad and toss. Sprinkle with Roquefort cheese, if desired. Serve immediately.

Makes: 4 servings
Nutrition Facts per serving: 82 cal., 7 g total fat (I g sat. fat),
0 mg chol., 85 mg sodium, 4 g carbo., 3 g fiber, 2 g pro.
Daily Values: 36% vit. A, 14% vit. C, 6% calcium, 5% iron

Red Wine Vinaigrette:
1. In a blender combine $1/3$ cup red wine vinegar, I tablespoon chopped fresh oregano, I teaspoon Dijon mustard, I teaspoon finely chopped shallot, $1/2$ teaspoon salt, black pepper, and I clove garlic. Pulse a few times to mix ingredients together. Let stand for a few minutes so the flavors will develop.

2. With the blender set to low and the lid on, start the blender. Remove the plug in the lid and very slowly add $2/3$ cup extra-virgin olive oil or canola oil in a fine stream. The mustard will cause the vinegar and oil to emulsify, and the vinaigrette will thicken. Turn off blender and let thicken. Season to taste.

Makes: I cup
Nutrition Facts per tablespoon: 81 cal., 9 g total fat (I g sat. fat),
0 mg chol., 80 mg sodium, 0 g carbo., 0 g fiber, 0 g pro.
Daily Values: 1% vit. C, 1% iron

44

The red wine vinegar, garlic, and oregano give this vinaigrette a real Italian taste. It's the dressing you're likely to get on your salad at a pizza parlor. Kids...pizza...do I need to tell you how much they love this?

oston Lettuce, Oranges, and Red Onion Salad with Ginger Dressing

This beautiful citrus salad is so light and refreshing, it's almost a palate cleanser. I've served it at fancy dinner parties and at school with equal success. The zing of the Ginger Dressing adds a whole new taste dimension.

1   head Boston lettuce

2   navel oranges

½   small red onion, thinly sliced

Ginger Dressing

Salt and black pepper

1. Prepare the Boston lettuce by breaking all the leaves apart and washing thoroughly under cold running water. Boston lettuce can be sandy inside, so be sure that the leaves are well washed. Dry the lettuce and tear into bite-size pieces. Place in a bowl and cover with damp towels. Store in the refrigerator until ready to use.

2. Prepare the oranges by peeling them and cutting into sections. More simply, slice the peeled oranges crosswise, then cut the slices in half.

3. Add the oranges and onion to the bowl with the lettuce. Pour some Ginger Dressing over the salad and toss. Season to taste with salt and pepper. Serve immediately. Pass remaining dressing, if you like.

Makes: 4 servings
Nutrition Facts per serving with Ginger Dressing: 75 cal.,5 g total fat
(1 g sat. fat), 0 mg chol., 278 mg sodium, 5 g carbo., 11 g fiber, 1 g pro.
Daily Values: 29% vit. A, 31% vit. C, 3% calcium, 4% iron

Ginger Dressing:
1. In a blender combine 3 tablespoons soy sauce, 3 tablespoons vinegar, 1 tablespoon finely chopped onion, 1 tablespoon grated fresh ginger, 1 tablespoon grated carrot, and 1 tablespoon honey. Pulse a few times to mix ingredients together. Let stand for a few minutes so the flavors will develop.

2. With the blender set to low and the lid on, start the blender. Remove the plug in the lid and very slowly add ½ cup vegetable oil in a fine stream. Turn off the blender and let thicken.

Makes: 1 cup
Nutrition Facts per tablespoon: 67 cal., 7 g total fat (1 g sat. fat),
0 mg chol., 173 mg sodium, 2 g carbo., 0 g fiber, 1 g pro.
Daily Values: 3% vit. A

Japanese restaurants often
serve Ginger Dressing.
Its strong flavors go over
surprisingly well with the kids.

Chef Bobo's Simple and Delicious Guacamole

The key to great guacamole is to keep it simple and make it fresh. If you want it really hot, add chopped habañero peppers instead of jalapeños. It took me years to create a recipe with just the right everything—taste, texture, zing. I promise you'll get raves every time you make it. Of course, you can serve it with tortilla chips, but try it as a dip for raw vegetables or as a garnish on black beans or black bean soup.

4 ripe Hass avocados*, seeded, peeled, and cut into chunks

¼ cup very finely chopped red onion

¼ cup very finely chopped fresh cilantro

2 fresh jalapeño chile peppers, seeded and finely chopped

1 lime, juiced (about 4 teaspoons)

   Hot pepper sauce

   Salt and black pepper

   Tortilla chips or fresh vegetable dippers (optional)

1. Use a fork or potato masher to mash the avocados, leaving them chunky. Stir in the red onion, cilantro, and jalapeño peppers.

2. Add lime juice and hot pepper sauce to taste. Mix well. Season to taste with salt and pepper. It should taste so good that you want to eat it all yourself.

3. If the guacamole has to sit for a few hours, push some of the avocado pits down into it. This will help keep the guacamole from oxidizing and turning brown. Cover with plastic wrap or put in an airtight container and store in the refrigerator. Serve with tortilla chips or fresh vegetables.

Makes: about 2 cups
*Note: Hass avocados are a dark-green, pebbly skinned variety of avocado grown in California and are available year-round. When purchasing, make sure they are soft enough just to yield to your touch. Hard avocados lack flavor.

Nutrition Facts per tablespoon: 39 cal., 4 g total fat (1 g sat. fat),
0 mg chol., 8 mg sodium, 2 g carbo., 1 g fiber, 1 g pro.
Daily Values: 4% vit. A, 4% vit. C, 1% calcium, 2% iron

omato, Red Onion, and Cilantro

A true summer taste: the sweetness of the tomatoes cut by the tang of cilantro and vinegar. This side is a natural to accompany something grilled—anything from chicken to fish or lamb. I actually like to serve this salad spooned directly on top of grilled meat. The vinegar brings out more of the flavor and the combination is sublime.

½ **pound ripe tomatoes***

½ **small red onion, thinly sliced or finely chopped**

¾ **cup fresh cilantro leaves**

Red wine vinegar

Extra-virgin olive oil or canola oil

Salt

Freshly ground black pepper

1. You can chop the tomatoes in chunks or slice them. If they are small cherry tomatoes, you can either quarter them or cut them in half—whatever way you like them. Place the tomatoes in a bowl, then add the red onion and cilantro.

2. Sprinkle just enough vinegar over the salad to give it a fresh taste. Then add a little olive oil by slowly drizzling it over the salad and toss. Season to taste with salt and pepper. Serve immediately.

Makes: 4 servings

***Note:** Use any kind of tomatoes that you like, as long as they are ripe, not hard.

Nutrition Facts per serving: 81 cal., 7 g total fat (1 g sat. fat),
0 mg chol., 159 mg sodium, 5 g carbo., 1 g fiber, 1 g pro.
Daily Values: 25% vit. A, 28% vit. C, 2% calcium, 3% iron

Tomato, Mozzarella, and Basil Salad

This sunny salad is one more reason to love summer. When I make it, I try to find different color tomatoes to make it even more striking. I also use part-skim mozzarella to keep it more healthful.

1 pound ripe tomatoes

½ pound part-skim mozzarella cheese

¼ cup finely shredded fresh basil

Extra-virgin olive oil or canola oil

Salt

Freshly ground black pepper

1. Preparing this salad is so simple and determined by how you and your family like to eat it. You can cut the tomatoes into wedges and cube the cheese. Or if you really want to dress up this dish, slice the tomatoes and the cheese and arrange them, alternating slices of tomato and cheese on a salad plate or a platter. Sprinkle the basil over the top. Finish it with a drizzle of a little olive oil and a sprinkle of salt and pepper.

Makes: 4 servings
Nutrition Facts per serving: 195 cal., 13 g total fat (6 g sat. fat), 32 mg chol., 416 mg sodium, 7 g carbo., 1 g fiber, 15 g pro.
Daily Values: 21% vit. A, 34% vit. C, 37% calcium, 4% iron

Expect smiling faces around your table when you serve this salad. If you're really in a hurry, cut the tomatoes into wedges, grate the cheese over the top, then add the basil, salt, and pepper and toss it all together.

Carrots and Raisin Salad

Shredded carrots and raisins make a comforting, slightly sweeter coleslaw. Kids adore it—no wonder! With just a little prep, one step, and one bowl to clean, you will too!

2 **large carrots, shredded**

½ **cup raisins**

¼ **cup chopped walnuts (optional)**

¼ **cup Honey-Mustard Vinaigrette (page 36)**

1. Combine carrots, raisins, and, if you like, walnuts in a bowl. Pour the Honey-Mustard Vinaigrette over salad and toss. Let stand about 30 minutes so that all the flavors come together.

Makes: 4 servings

Nutrition Facts per serving: 154 cal., 7 g total fat (1 g sat. fat), 0 mg chol., 111 mg sodium, 23 g carbo., 2 g fiber, 1 g pro.
Daily Values: 256% vit. A, 8% vit. C, 2% calcium, 4% iron

I think of every kitchen as a center of community, just as it is at Calhoun. It's a wonderful place to communicate, discover, and share life.

soups

garden variety

Want a foolproof way to get your kids to eat their broccoli and spinach? It's this simple. Soup teaches kids to eat vegetables. These kid-tested winners are warm, welcoming, and positively electric with wonderful flavors.

 # **B**asic Vegetable Stock

This is the basis of all of our soups in this book. I like to make double batches and keep them stored in my freezer in 2-cup portions so I always have stock when I want to make soup. It will keep in the refrigerator for up to one week.

2 tablespoons vegetable oil

3 small turnips,
coarsely chopped

2 stalks celery,
coarsely chopped

1 large onion,
coarsely chopped

1 leek (white part only),
halved lengthwise and
coarsely chopped

1 large carrot,
coarsely chopped

8 cups water

1. Heat oil in a 3-quart soup pot over high heat until hot. Add turnips, celery, onion, leek, and carrot. Stir the vegetables around until they begin to cook but don't turn brown.

2. Add water to stock pot. Bring to a boil. Reduce heat to simmering and cook until the vegetables are very soft, about 2 hours. Remove pot from heat. Let cool. Strain and discard the vegetables.

3. Store the cooled and strained stock in an airtight container in the refrigerator. It also can be stored in small quantities in the freezer for up to 3 months.

Makes: 8 cups

# Three Onion Soup

What separates a decent onion soup from an outstanding one is the caramelizing of the onions. The more caramelization, the more flavorful the soup will be. This one is sweet, dark brown, and heavenly. Serve it with a crunchy baguette.

2 tablespoons vegetable oil

2 medium yellow onions, thinly sliced

2 medium red onions, thinly sliced

6 shallots, halved and thinly sliced

¼ cup white wine vinegar

2 tablespoons Worcestershire sauce

2 tablespoons all-purpose flour

5 cups Basic Vegetable Stock (page 56)

1 teaspoon dried thyme, crushed

2 bay leaves

¼ cup dry white wine or 2 tablespoons dry white vermouth (optional)

   Salt and black pepper

1. Drizzle the oil in a nonstick skillet large enough to hold all of the onions and swirl it around until the oil coats the entire surface. Heat over high heat until hot. Add yellow onions, red onions, and shallots. Reduce heat to medium. Let the onions cook down, stirring constantly to keep them from scorching on the bottom. It will take about 15 minutes for the onions to start to brown and at least another 15 minutes to get a deep caramelization. The onions will reduce in volume significantly as you cook the moisture out of them. (While you start out with a skillet full of onions, the finished product will cover just the bottom of the skillet.) When the onions are a deep shade of brown, add the vinegar and Worcestershire sauce. Cook until the liquid has evaporated. Sift the flour over the onions and stir to coat. Cook for 2 or 3 minutes or until thickened.

2. Transfer the onions to a 3-quart soup pot. Add the Basic Vegetable Stock, thyme, and bay leaves. Simmer over medium heat for 15 minutes, stirring occasionally. If you like, stir in the wine and cook 1 minute more. Season to taste with salt and pepper. Remove bay leaves before serving.

Makes: 4 servings
Nutrition Facts per serving: 197 cal., 8 g total fat (1 g sat. fat),
0 mg chol., 585 mg sodium, 27 g carbo., 2 g fiber, 6 g pro.
Daily Values: 21% vit. A, 17% vit. C, 5% calcium, 12% iron

Chunky Vegetable Soup

At Calhoun, this is the soup we often make at the end of the week so we can use up our fresh vegetables. Part of the charm is that you never know how it's going to taste from one time to the next. And lest this sound like a random free-for-all, trust me: the flavors become harmonious as it slowly simmers.

¼ cup olive oil

2 red bliss potatoes, chopped

1 onion, chopped

1 stalk celery, chopped

1 leek (white part only), halved lengthwise and chopped

1 turnip, chopped

1 carrot, chopped

¼ cup chopped shallots

3 cloves garlic, minced

4 cups Basic Vegetable Stock (see page 56)

Bouquet Garni I

5 zucchini, chopped

2 cups chopped plum tomatoes

1 yellow summer squash, chopped

1 cup green beans, cut into 1-inch pieces

¼ teaspoon red wine vinegar

Fine sea salt

Freshly ground black pepper

1. Heat oil in a 3-quart soup pot over high heat until hot. Add potatoes, onion, celery, leek, turnip, carrot, shallots, and garlic. Stir the vegetables around until they begin to cook but don't turn brown.

2. Add the Basic Vegetable Stock and the Bouquet Garni I to soup pot. Bring to a boil. Reduce heat to simmering and cook for 45 minutes.

3. Add the zucchini, tomatoes, summer squash, and green beans to soup pot. Simmer 15 minutes more. Stir in the vinegar. Season to taste with salt and pepper. If the soup is too thick, stir in a little water or more Basic Vegetable Stock.

Bouquet Garni I: Bundle 3 sprigs fresh thyme, 3 sprigs fresh parsley, 1 bay leaf, and 1 tablespoon black peppercorns together in several thicknesses of cotton cheesecloth. Tie closed with string.

Makes: 4 to 6 servings
Nutrition Facts per serving: 311 cal., 15 g total fat (2 g sat. fat),
0 mg chol., 342 mg sodium, 41 g carbo., 8 g fiber, 10 g pro.
Daily Values: 118% vit. A, 107% vit. C, 10% calcium, 20% iron

If you prepare a double batch of the Basic Vegetable Stock on the weekend and freeze it in 2-cup portions, this soup is a simple weeknight meal—and easily taylored to meet your family's vegetable preferences.

58

Carrot-Ginger Soup

This bright, velvety soup gets a delicious wake-up call from fresh ginger and ground ginger. Here, carrots are anything but ordinary—they absolutely shine.

2 tablespoons extra-virgin olive oil or canola oil

1 medium onion, chopped

¼ cup chopped shallots

2 bay leaves

2 cloves garlic, minced

4 medium carrots, chopped

1 tablespoon grated fresh ginger

1 tablespoon kosher salt

1 tablespoon turbinado sugar or regular sugar

2 teaspoons ground white pepper

4 cups Basic Vegetable Stock (page 56)

1 teaspoon ground ginger

1. Drizzle the oil in a heavy 3-quart soup pot and swirl it around until the oil coats the entire surface. Heat over high heat until hot.

2. Add the onion, shallots, bay leaves, and garlic. Cook and stir until tender but not brown.

3. Add the carrots, fresh ginger, salt, sugar, and pepper. Stir in the Basic Vegetable Stock. Bring to a boil. Reduce heat to simmering and cook until carrots are tender, about 45 minutes. Remove soup pot from heat. Cool for 15 minutes.

4. Ladle soup into a blender a little at a time and blend in small batches until pureed. (Be very careful because hot liquids in a blender can be explosive when you turn on the blender.) Once all the soup is blended, return soup to pot. Or use an immersion blender to blend the soup right in the soup pot.

5. Top each serving with a sprinkling of ground ginger.

Makes: 4 to 6 servings

Nutrition Facts per serving: 151 cal., 8 g total fat (1 g sat. fat), 0 mg chol., 1,503 mg sodium, 20 g carbo., 3 g fiber, 4 g pro.
Daily Values: 316% vit. A, 13% vit. C, 4% calcium, 6% iron

# C arrot, Fennel, and Coconut Soup

Using both fresh fennel and fennel seeds means the fennel flavor melds with other taste notes and becomes so beautifully integrated that kids immediately take to the distinctively licorce-y taste. Because it uses coconut milk, it's good for anyone who's lactose intolerant.

2 tablespoons extra-virgin olive oil or canola oil

1 teaspoon fennel seeds, crushed

1 teaspoon ground coriander

4 medium carrots, cut into ½-inch pieces

2 fennel bulbs*, cut into ½-inch slices

1 onion, cut into ½ inch slices

1 leek (white part only), halved lengthwise and cut ½ inch thick

3 cloves garlic, smashed

4 cups Basic Vegetable Stock (see page 56) or water

Bouquet Garni 2

1 12-ounce can unsweetened coconut milk

1 lime, juiced (about 4 teaspoons)

1 tablespoon brown sugar

2 teaspoons salt

Black pepper

1. Drizzle 1 tablespoon of the oil in a 3-quart soup pot and swirl it around until the oil coats the entire surface. Heat over medium heat until hot. Add the fennel seeds and coriander. Cook and stir until fragrant, about 1 minute. Add the remaining 1 tablespoon oil to soup pot. Add the carrots, fennel, onion, leek, and garlic. Stir the vegetables around until they begin to cook but don't turn brown.

2. Add the Basic Vegetable Stock or water and the Bouquet Garni 2 to soup pot. Bring to a boil. Reduce heat to simmering and cook, covered, until the vegetables are falling-apart soft, about 45 minutes. Remove soup pot from heat. Cool 15 minutes.

3. Remove Bouquet Garni 2. Ladle soup into a blender a little bit at a time and blend in small batches until smooth. (Be very careful because hot liquids in a blender can be explosive when you turn on the blender.) Once all the soup is blended, return soup to soup pot. Stir in the coconut milk, lime juice, brown sugar, and salt. Season to taste with pepper. Heat through.

*Note: Fennel is also called anise and resembles something like an onion with green, celerylike stalks on top. It smells faintly of licorice. To clean fennel bulbs, cut off and discard the long green stalks first(some grocers already remove these stalks). Using a vegetable peeler, peel the outside layers of the fennel, which contain stringy filaments like you find in tough celery. Cut the bulb in half and slice it like you would slice an onion, discarding the small brown root portion at the end.

Bouquet Garni 2: Bundle 8 sprigs fresh thyme, 2 bay leaves, and 1 tablespoon black peppercorns together in several thicknesses of cotton cheesecloth. Tie closed with string.

Makes: 8 servings

Nutrition Facts per serving: 155 cal., 12 g total fat (8 g sat. fat), 0 mg chol., 704 mg sodium, 12 g carbo., 7 g fiber, 3 g pro. Daily Values: 156% vit. A, 11% vit. C, 3% calcium, 5% iron

iso Soup

The classic soup that's served in every Japanese restaurant, Miso Soup is more familiar than foreign. It's intensely flavorful and healthful. The miso (fermented soy paste) and silken tofu (made from the curds of soy milk) prove you don't have to serve meat to get the protein you need.

2 cups Basic Vegetable Stock (page 56)

1 tablespoon chopped fresh lemongrass*

1 1-inch piece fresh ginger, peeled and grated

1 shallot, minced

1 clove garlic, minced

5 dried shiitake mushrooms

1 small carrot, cut into short, very thin strips

1 3-inch piece diakon, cut into short, very thin strips

1 to 2 tablespoons soy sauce

¼ teaspoon toasted sesame oil

1 cup red or white miso (fermented bean paste)

4 sheets nori paper, cut into strips

½ cup firm silken tofu, cut into small cubes (optional)

Finely chopped scallions

1. In a 3-quart soup pot combine the Basic Vegetable Stock, lemongrass, ginger, shallot, and garlic. Bring to a boil. Reduce heat to simmering and cook for 30 minutes to extract flavors. Pour through a strainer, discarding the solids. Return stock to soup pot.

2. Meanwhile, pour 2 cups boiling water over the shiitake mushrooms. Soak for 30 minutes. Remove mushrooms from the water and cut them into short, very thin strips. Strain the soaking water through a coffee filter to remove any dirt, reserving the soaking water.

3. Measure the reserved soaking water, mushrooms, carrot, daikon, soy sauce, and sesame oil; add enough water to make 8 cups. Add all to soup pot. Bring to a boil. Remove from heat.

4. In a bowl whisk together the miso and 1 cup of the soup liquid until no lumps remain. Add it to the soup pot. After adding the miso to the soup, don't bring the soup back to a boil. Miso is fermented soybean paste, and the healthful bacteria in the soup will be killed. Add the nori and, if you like, the tofu. Let stand about 10 minutes or until the nori is soft. Top each serving with scallions.

*Note: If you don't have fresh lemongrass, a small squeeze of lemon at the end adds a nice freshness to the soup.

Makes: 4 servings
Nutrition Facts per serving: 190 cal., 5 g total fat (1 g sat. fat),
0 mg chol., 2,769 mg sodium, 27 g carbo., 6 g fiber, 12 g pro.
Daily Values: 70% vit. A, 23% vit. C, 6% calcium, 13% iron

Miso Soup, mysterious and intensely flavored, is the perfect way to introduce kids to soy foods.

Music to my ears...

We've made definite headway at Calhoun. Now, kids and parents ask me for recipes. Third graders are making their own vinaigrettes and pizzas at home. A fourth grader asked for a Cuisinart for Christmas. And there are two things I hear over and over—both are music to my ears: "Chef Bobo, could I please have a little bit of everything?" and "I never thought my child would eat Cream of Cauliflower Soup."

Chef Bobo's Cream of Cauliflower Soup

This is one of the first soups I served when I started at Calhoun, and I think of it as the recipe that let us know we were on the right track. When the kids—even the non-vegetable lovers—tried it, they were seduced by its delicately seasoned flavor. Parents were shocked (and thrilled) when their kids started asking for the recipe. This, I'm proud to add, is the recipe that is immortalized on the National Public Radio website!

2 tablespoons olive oil

1 medium onion, chopped

5 cups cauliflower florets

2 cups Basic Vegetable Stock (page 56)

1 cup milk

½ teaspoon ground coriander

Salt and black pepper

Milk

2 tablespoons chopped fresh parsley or chives

1. Drizzle oil in a large saucepan and swirl it around until the oil coats the entire surface of the bottom of the pan. Heat over medium-high heat until hot. Add the onions. Cook and stir until tender. Immediately stir in the cauliflower.

2. Add the Basic Vegetable Stock, milk, and coriander. Season to taste with salt and pepper. Bring to a boil. Reduce heat to simmering and cook until cauliflower is tender and easy to cut, 25 to 30 minutes. Cool 15 minutes.

3. Ladle soup into a blender a little at a time and blend until smooth. (Be very careful because hot liquids in a blender can be explosive when you turn the blender on.) Once all the soup is blended, return soup to saucepan. Or use an immersion blender to blend the soup right in the saucepan. If soup is too thick, stir in a little more milk until you have a nice creamy consistency.

4. Top each serving with parsley or chives.

Makes: 4 to 6 servings
Nutrition Facts per serving: 141 cal., 9 g total fat (2 g sat. fat),
5 mg chol., 373 mg sodium, 13 g carbo., 4 g fiber, 6 g pro.
Daily Values: 7% vit. A, 84% vit. C, 11% calcium, 4% iron

Tomato and Basil Soup

A tomato soup that is basic but not boring! The tomato and fresh basil combination makes the most of two great natural flavors. This is one of my favorites served with a grilled cheese sandwich.

2 tablespoons extra-virgin olive oil or canola oil

1 medium onion, chopped

1 medium carrot, chopped

1 stalk celery, chopped

2 teaspoons chopped fresh oregano

2 bay leaves

2 cloves garlic, minced

2 28-ounce cans whole Italian-style tomatoes, undrained

1 cup Basic Vegetable Stock (page 56)

2 teaspoons kosher salt

1 cup fresh basil leaves, chopped

Shaved Parmesan cheese (optional)

1. Drizzle the oil in a heavy 3-quart soup pot and swirl it around until the oil coats the entire surface. Heat over high heat until hot.

2. Add the onion, carrot, celery, oregano, bay leaves, and garlic. Cook and stir until tender but not brown.

3. Add the undrained tomatoes, the Basic Vegetable Stock, and salt. Bring to a boil. Reduce heat to simmering and cook for 45 minutes. Remove soup pot from heat. Stir in half of the basil. Cool for 15 minutes.

4. Ladle soup into a blender a little at a time and blend until pureed. (Be very careful because hot liquids in a blender can be explosive when you turn on the blender.) Once all the soup is blended, return soup to pot. Or use an immersion blender to blend the soup right in the soup pot.

5. Sprinkle each serving with some of the remaining basil. If you like, top with Parmesan cheese.

Makes: 4 to 6 servings

Nutrition Facts per serving: 164 cal., 8 g total fat (1 g sat. fat), 0 mg chol., 1,579 mg sodium, 23 g carbo., 6 g fiber, 5 g pro.
Daily Values: 135% vit. A, 105% vit. C, 16% calcium, 17% iron

Much improved from a processed, canned tomato soup, your kids will insist on homemade every time. Use an immersion blender to make it as smooth or chunky as your family desires.

P *otato and Leek Soup*

Showcasing just two ingredients, this classic soup brings out the best in both. Thick and homey, just the smell of it cooking is enough to make you hungry.

2 tablespoons butter or olive oil

6 large leeks (white parts only), halved lengthwise and cut ½ inch thick

3 medium baking potatoes, thinly sliced

1 medium onion, thinly sliced

2 cloves garlic, minced

6 cups Basic Vegetable Stock (page 56)

   Bouquet Garni 2 (page 61)

2 teaspoons salt

½ cup dry white wine (optional)

   Black pepper

1. Melt butter in a 3-quart soup pot and swirl it around until it coats the entire surface. Heat over high heat for 1 minute. Add the leeks, potatoes, onion, and garlic. Cook and stir until leeks and onion are tender, about 5 minutes.

2. Add the Basic Vegetable Stock and Bouquet Garni 2. Bring to a boil. Reduce heat to simmering and cook for 30 minutes. Remove pot from heat. Cool for 15 minutes.

3. Remove Bouquet Garni 2. Use an immersion blender to puree soup right in the soup pot. Stir in salt. If you like, stir in white wine. Cook 5 minutes more. Season to taste with pepper.

Makes: 4 to 6 servings
Nutrition Facts per serving: 202 cal., 8 g total fat (4 g sat. fat),
16 mg chol., 1,307 mg sodium, 32 g carbo., 3 g fiber, 6 g pro.
Daily Values: 12% vit. A, 34% vit. C, 5% calcium, 12% iron

Curried Cauliflower Soup

By introducing the sweetly pungent flavor and fragrance of curry, cauliflower blooms (pun intended) into a soup that is as delectable as it is beautiful. It's a great way to expand your kids' taste buds and entice them to eat vegetables at the same time!

2 tablespoons extra-virgin olive oil or canola oil

1 tablespoon curry powder

2 pounds cauliflower florets

2 stalks celery, chopped

1 medium carrot, chopped

1 onion, chopped

1 leek (white part only), halved lengthwise and cut ½ inch thick

3 cloves garlic, smashed

4 cups Basic Vegetable Stock (page 56) or water

2 tablespoons white wine vinegar

Bouquet Garni 2 (page 61)

Salt and black pepper

1. Drizzle oil in a 3-quart soup pot and swirl it around until the oil coats the entire surface. Heat over high heat until hot. Add the curry powder. Cook and stir until fragrant, about 30 seconds. Add the cauliflower, celery, carrot, onion, leek, and garlic. Stir the vegetables around until they begin to cook but don't turn brown.

2. Add the Basic Vegetable Stock or water, vinegar, and Bouquet Garni 2. Bring to a boil. Reduce heat to simmering and cook until vegetables are falling-apart soft, about 30 minutes. Remove soup pot from heat. Cool 15 minutes. Remove Bouquet Garni 2.

3. Use an immersion blender to puree the soup right in the soup pot. Season to taste with salt and pepper. Check the soup for consistency. If soup is too thick, stir in a little water or more Basic Vegetable Stock.

Makes: 4 servings
Nutrition Facts per serving: 171 cal., 9 g total fat (1 g sat. fat),
 0 mg chol., 860 mg sodium, 22 g carbo., 7 g fiber, 8 g pro.
Daily Values: 83% vit. A, 159% vit. C, 9% calcium, 11% iron

# Corn Chowder with Fresh Basil

When you think chowder, you typically think winter. This chowder is the exception to the seasonal rule. It's a summery taste treat that sparkles with the addition of fresh basil. If you have fresh corn, by all means use that.

2 tablespoons extra-virgin olive oil or canola oil

1 teaspoon ground ginger

2 stalks celery, chopped

1 carrot, chopped

1 onion, chopped

1 leek (white part only), halved lengthwise and chopped

1 baking potato, chopped

3 cloves garlic, smashed

1 16-ounce bag frozen corn, thawed

4 cups Basic Vegetable Stock (page 56) or water

2 tablespoons dry sherry or red wine vinegar

Bouquet Garni 2 (page 61)

2 teaspoons salt

Black pepper

2 small bunches fresh basil, chopped (1½ cups)

1. Drizzle oil in a 3-quart soup pot and swirl it around until the oil coats the entire surface. Heat over high heat until hot. Add the ginger. Cook and stir until fragrant, about 30 seconds. Add the celery, carrot, onion, leek, potato, and garlic. Stir the vegetables around until they begin to cook but don't turn brown.

2. Stir in the corn. Cook 5 minutes more, stirring often to avoid burning the vegetables on the bottom. Add the Basic Vegetable Stock, dry sherry or vinegar, and Bouquet Garni 2. Bring to a boil. Reduce heat to simmering and cook for 45 minutes. Remove soup pot from heat. Cool 15 minutes. Remove Bouquet Garni 2. Strain out 1 cup of the vegetables; set aside.

3. Use an immersion blender to puree the rest of the soup right in the soup pot until creamy but with some chunks of corn still visible. Return the reserved vegetables to the soup pot. Stir in salt to taste. Season to taste with pepper. Stir in basil. Heat through.

Southwest Corn Chowder:
For a spicier version of this soup, stir in 2 tablespoons chopped fresh cilantro; ½ of a fresh jalapeño chile pepper, seeded and chopped; and several dashes hot pepper sauce. If you like, sprinkle each serving with a little bit of shredded cheddar cheese.

Makes: 4 to 6 servings

Nutrition Facts per serving: 250 cal., 9 g total fat (1 g sat. fat), 0 mg chol., 1,185 mg sodium, 41 g carbo., 4 g fiber, 7 g pro.
Daily Values: 84% vit. A, 29% vit. C, 4% calcium, 8% iron

It's a good thing our recipes are healthful because the kitchen team spends a lot of time taste-testing!

Corn Chowder

The milk and potatoes are what make this a chowder, not a soup. Chowders traditionally say "comfort and warmth." This one is hearty and colorful—flecked with red peppers, bright carrots, and golden corn.

¼ cup olive oil

4 red bliss potatoes, chopped

2 red bell peppers, chopped

1 onion, chopped

1 stalk celery, chopped

1 leek (white part only), halved lengthwise and chopped

1 carrot, chopped

¼ cup chopped shallots

3 cloves garlic, minced

4 cups Basic Vegetable Stock (page 56)

Bouquet Garni I (page 58)

4 cups fresh or frozen corn

1 teaspoon fresh lime juice

Fine sea salt

Freshly ground black pepper

1. Drizzle oil in a 3-quart soup pot and swirl it around until the oil coats the entire surface. Heat over high heat until hot. Add potatoes, bell peppers, onion, celery, leek, carrot, shallots, and garlic. Stir around the vegetables until they begin to cook but don't turn brown.

2. Stir in the Basic Vegetable Stock and Bouquet Garni I. Bring to a boil. Reduce heat to simmering and cook for 45 minutes. Add corn. Simmer 15 minutes more. Stir in lime juice. Season to taste with salt and pepper. Check the soup for consistency. If soup is too thick, add a little more Basic Vegetable Stock or water.

Makes: 4 servings

Nutrition Facts per serving: 424 cal., 16 g total fat (2 g sat. fat), 0 mg chol., 457 mg sodium, 69 g carbo., 7 g fiber, 11 g pro.
Daily Values: 159% vit. A, 215% vit. C, 6% calcium, 18% iron

 **ream of Broccoli Soup**

A gently spiced soup, this is a great way to get kids to eat broccoli. This soup doesn't just taste good, it looks lovely. When it's pureed, you get a spring green color and creamy texture.

2 tablespoons olive oil

1 medium onion, chopped

5 cups broccoli florets

3 cups Basic Vegetable Stock (page 56)

½ teaspoon ground coriander

½ teaspoon ground nutmeg

Salt and black pepper

½ teaspoon red wine vinegar

1. Drizzle oil in a 3-quart soup pot and swirl it around until the oil coats the entire surface. Heat over medium-high heat until hot. Add the onion. Cook and stir until tender. Immediately stir in the broccoli.

2. Add the Basic Vegetable Stock, coriander, and nutmeg. Season to taste with salt and pepper. Bring to a boil. Reduce heat to simmering and cook until broccoli is tender and easy to cut, 25 to 30 minutes. Cool 15 minutes.

3. Ladle soup into a blender a little at a time and blend in small batches until smooth. (Be very careful because hot liquids in a blender can be explosive when you turn on the blender.) Once all the soup is blended, return soup to saucepan. Or use an immersion blender to blend the soup right in the saucepan. If soup is too thick, stir in a little water or more Basic Vegetable Stock until you have a nice creamy consistency. Stir in the vinegar.

Makes: 4 to 6 servings
Nutrition Facts per serving: 115 cal., 8 g total fat (1 g sat. fat),
0 mg chol., 344 mg sodium, 10 g carbo., 4 g fiber, 5 g pro.
Daily Values: 35% vit. A, 147% vit. C, 6% calcium, 6% iron

 **O**ven-Roasted Red Pepper Soup

The roasting and peeling of the peppers mean you'll put some effort in, but this soup's well worth it. The sweet peppers are nicely balanced by the vibrant jolt of vinegar and hot pepper sauce.

8 red bell peppers
   Vegetable oil

2 tablespoons extra-virgin olive oil or canola oil

1 tablespoon mild or spicy paprika

1 teaspoon ground coriander

2 stalks celery, chopped into ½-inch pieces

1 medium carrot, chopped into ½-inch pieces

1 onion, chopped into ½-inch pieces

1 leek (white part only), halved lengthwise and cut ½ inch thick

5 cloves garlic, smashed

4 cups Basic Vegetable Stock (page 56) or water

1 tablespoon white wine vinegar

1 tablespoon balsamic vinegar

2 to 3 dashes hot pepper sauce
   Bouquet Garni 2 (page 61)

2 teaspoons salt
   Black pepper

1. To roast bell peppers, preheat broiler. Meanwhile, cut each bell pepper in half lengthwise, remove the core and seeds, and rub it with vegetable oil. Place the peppers, skin sides up, on a greased baking sheet. Broil the peppers for 10 to 15 minutes or until the skin is blackened and crackly, turning once so they roast all around. Remove from broiler. Let cool in a bowl covered with plastic wrap for 15 minutes. After that, you should be able to peel the skin easily off the peppers. Cut 4 of the roasted pepper halves into short, thin strips. Set aside.

2. Drizzle the 2 tablespoons olive oil in a 3-quart soup pot; swirl to coat entire bottom of pan with oil. Heat over medium heat for 1 minute. Add the paprika and coriander. Cook and stir until fragrant, about 30 seconds. Add the remaining roasted pepper halves, celery, carrot, onion, leek, and garlic to soup pot. Cook and stir for 5 minutes.

3. Add the Basic Vegetable Stock or water, white wine vinegar, balsamic vinegar, hot pepper sauce, and Bouquet Garni 2 to soup pot. Bring to a boil. Reduce heat to simmer and cook until the vegetables are falling-apart soft, about 30 minutes. Remove pot from heat. Cool 15 minutes.

4. Remove the Bouquet Garni 2. Ladle soup into a blender a little at a time and blend until smooth. (Be very careful because hot liquids in a blender can be explosive when you turn the blender on.) Once all the soup is blended, return soup to soup pot. Or use an immersion blender to blend the soup right in the soup pot. If soup is too thick, stir in a little water or more Basic Vegetable Stock. Stir in the salt. Season to taste with pepper. Stir in the reserved roasted pepper slices.

Makes: 4 to 6 servings
Nutrition Facts per serving: 218 cal., 12 g total fat (1 g sat. fat), 0 mg chol., 1,269 mg sodium, 27 g carbo., 7 g fiber, 5 g pro.
Daily Values: 354% vit. A, 651% vit. C, 6% calcium, 11% iron

It's this simple. If you want your kids to eat vegetables, make vegetable soups. For the blended soup recipes, we puree them until nearly smooth, as the kids tend to like them better that way.

Split Pea Soup

Finally, pea soup is rescued from its unhappy reputation as a dense green-brown school-cafeteria staple that hasn't changed since 1930. It's lively and beautifully balanced, enhanced with fresh herbs and a splash of lemon.

1 tablespoon extra-virgin olive or canola oil

2 stalks celery, chopped

1 medium carrot, chopped

1 medium onion, chopped

1 leek (white part only), halved lengthwise and cut ½ inch thick

4 cloves garlic, smashed

1 recipe Basic Vegetable Stock (page 56) or water

2 cups dry split peas, rinsed and drained

  Bouquet Garni 2 (page 61)

¼ pound thick bacon, cooked and crumbled; smoked ham, chopped; or several dashes liquid smoke (optional)

1 lemon, juiced (about 4 teaspoons)

2 teaspoons salt

1 teaspoon grated lemon zest

1. Drizzle oil in a 3-quart soup pot and swirl it around until the oil coats the entire surface of the bottom of the pan. Heat over high heat for 1 minute. Add the celery, carrot, onion, leek, and garlic. Cook and stir until onion and leek are tender, about 5 minutes.

2. Add the Basic Vegetable Stock or water, split peas, and Bouquet Garni 2. If you like, add the bacon. Bring to a boil. Reduce heat to simmering and cook for 45 to 60 minutes, stirring occasionally. Stir in lemon juice, salt, and lemon zest. Season to taste with pepper.

Makes: 4 to 6 servings
Nutrition Facts per serving: 489 cal., 7 g total fat (1 g sat. fat), 0 mg chol., 1,307 mg sodium, 82 g carbo., 31 g fiber, 33 g pro.
Daily Values: 89% vit. A, 26% vit. C, 9% calcium, 27% iron

At The Calhoun School, you will find my talented team working very hard, but there is always laughter as we lovingly prepare meals for some very special people.

 **lack Bean Soup**

The distinctive flavors of oregano, cumin, and garlic shine through this classic Latin American bean soup. Red vinegar and hot pepper sauce add an extra kick. If you want to make it creamy, take out a cup of the beans and puree them in a blender, then stir back into the soup.

1 pound dry black beans
2 tablespoons olive oil
2 teaspoons ground cumin
1 medium onion, chopped
1 green bell pepper, chopped
1 teaspoon black pepper
6 sprigs fresh oregano or
 1 teaspoon dried oregano, crushed
2 bay leaves
3 cloves garlic, minced
1 recipe Basic Vegetable Stock (page 56)
½ teaspoon hot pepper sauce
 Salt
1 teaspoon red wine vinegar
1 cup light sour cream
½ cup chopped scallions

1. Rinse beans. In a 3-quart soup pot combine beans and 8 cups cold water. Put the beans aside and let sit overnight. (This will make the beans less gaseous, and they will cook faster.) Or you may combine the beans and 8 cups cold water. Bring to a boil. Reduce heat and simmer 2 minutes. Remove soup pot from heat. Let stand for 1 hour. Drain and rinse.

2. Drizzle oil in a 3-quart soup pot and swirl it around until the oil coats the entire surface of the bottom of the pan. Heat over high heat until hot. Add cumin. Cook and stir until fragrant, about 30 seconds.

3. Add the onion, bell pepper, black pepper, oregano, bay leaves, and garlic. Stir so that the vegetables cook evenly and the flavors mingle. When the vegetables just begin to turn brown, stir in the drained beans, the Basic Vegetable Stock, and the hot pepper sauce. Bring to a boil. Reduce heat to simmering and cook, covered, for 1 ½ hours, stirring occasionally to make sure there are no beans sticking to the bottom.

4. Check the beans to see if they are fully cooked. They should be firm with no hard core. If so, the beans are done. Season to taste with salt. (You should never season beans with salt before or during cooking because doing so will make the beans tough.) Season with a little more pepper, if desired. Remove oregano sprigs and bay leaves. Stir in the red wine vinegar before serving.

5. Check soup for consistency. If the soup is too thick, add a little water. (The soup will thicken as it stands.) Top each serving with some of the sour cream and scallions.

Makes: 6 servings
Nutrition Facts per serving: 398 cal., 11 g total fat (3 g sat. fat), 13 mg chol., 1,370 mg sodium, 58 g carbo., 13 g fiber, 23g pro.
Daily Values: 15% vit. A, 31% vit. C, 18% calcium, 19% iron

Red Bean Soup

These are the beans you usually use for chili or stews, but here they're the basis for an earthy, unfussy soup. It couldn't be easier to make—the only real time invested is soaking the beans overnight and occasionally stirring while it slowly cooks. Kids and beans are a winning combination. When we tried this soup at Calhoun, the younger kids almost cleaned us out of it!

1   pound dry red kidney beans

2   tablespoons olive oil

1   stalk celery, finely chopped

1   medium onion, finely chopped

1   green bell pepper, finely chopped

1   teaspoon black pepper

5   sprigs fresh thyme or 1 teaspoon dried thyme, crushed

3   bay leaves

2   sprigs fresh oregano or 1 teaspoon dried oregano, crushed

2   cloves garlic, minced

1   recipe Basic Vegetable Stock (page 56)

1   tablespoon tomato paste

½   teaspoon hot pepper sauce

    Salt

    Hot pepper sauce (optional)

1. Rinse beans. In a 3-quart soup pot combine beans and 8 cups cold water. Put the beans aside and let sit overnight. (This will make the beans less gaseous and cook faster when ready to cook.) Or you may combine the beans and 8 cups cold water. Bring to a boil. Reduce heat and simmer 2 minutes. Remove soup pot from heat. Let stand for 1 hour. Drain and rinse.

2. Drizzle oil in a 3-quart soup pot and swirl it around until the oil coats the entire surface. Heat over high heat until hot. Add the celery, onion, bell pepper, black pepper, thyme, bay leaves, oregano, and garlic. Stir around so that the vegetables cook evenly and the flavors mingle. When the vegetables just begin to turn brown, stir in the drained beans, the Basic Vegetable Stock, tomato paste, and hot pepper sauce. Bring to a boil. Reduce heat to simmering and cook, covered, for 1½ hours, stirring occasionally to make sure there are no beans sticking to the bottom.

3. Check the beans to see if they are fully cooked. They should be firm with no hard core. If so, the beans are done. Season to taste with salt. (You should never season beans with salt before or during cooking because doing so will make the beans tough.) If desired, season with a little more pepper. Remove thyme and oregano sprigs and bay leaves. Cool for 15 minutes.

4. Ladle soup into a blender a little at a time and blend until smooth. (Be very careful because hot liquids in a blender can be explosive when you turn on the blender.) Once all the soup is blended, return soup to soup pot. Or use an immersion blender to blend the soup right in the soup pot.

5. Check the soup for consistency. If soup is too thick, add a little water. (The soup will thicken as it stands.) If desired, sprinkle each serving with additional hot pepper sauce.

Makes: 4 to 6 servings

Nutrition Facts per serving: 502 cal., 9 g total fat (1 g sat. fat), 0 mg chol., 1,255 mg sodium, 80 g carbo., 30 g fiber, 33 g pro. Daily Values: 14% vit. A, 52% vit. C, 22% calcium, 52% iron

Red Lentil Soup

We cook red lentils because of their golden, lighter color. French lentils are good too, but while they start out green they eventually turn brown. While French lentils make a good winter soup, perhaps red ones are better for spring. Technically, either type of lentil works.

2 tablespoons extra-virgin olive oil or canola oil

1 teaspoon ground cumin

½ teaspoon ground coriander

2 stalks celery, chopped

1 medium carrot, chopped

1 medium onion, chopped

1 leek (white part only), halved lengthwise and cut ½ inch thick

6 cloves garlic, smashed

1 recipe Basic Vegetable Stock (page 56)

2 cups water

2 cups red lentils, rinsed and drained

Bouquet Garni 2 (page 61)

1 lemon, juiced (about 4 teaspoons)

2 teaspoons salt

1 teaspoon grated lemon zest

Black pepper

1. Drizzle oil in a 3-quart soup pot and swirl it around until the oil coats the entire surface of the bottom of the pan. Heat over high heat for 1 minute. Add cumin and coriander. Cook and stir until fragrant, about 30 seconds. Add the celery, carrot, onion, leek, and garlic. Cook and stir until onion and leek are tender, about 5 minutes.

2. Add the Basic Vegetable Stock, water, lentils, and Bouquet Garni 2. Bring to a boil. Reduce heat to simmering and cook for 45 to 60 minutes, stirring occasionally. Stir in lemon juice, salt, and lemon zest. Remove Bouquet Garni 2. Season to taste with pepper.

Makes: 6 servings
Nutrition Facts per serving: 351 cal., 6 g total fat (1 g sat. fat),
0 mg chol., 1,221 mg sodium, 56 g carbo., 13 g fiber, 23 g pro.
Daily Values: 59% vit. A, 15% vit. C, 8% calcium, 23% iron

Our kids tend to love any type of bean or lentil soup. We use the red lentils here because their texture seems to be lighter.

# White Bean Soup

A spoonful of pesto sauce adds a burst of fresh flavor to this mellow soup. It's even better if you add the chunks of smoked sausage, country ham, or sweet Italian sausage.

1 pound dry cannellini (white kidney) beans

2 tablespoons olive oil

3 stalks celery, chopped

1 medium onion, chopped

½ fennel bulb, chopped (see note, page 61)

1 teaspoon black pepper

6 sprigs fresh parsley

2 bay leaves

1 clove garlic, minced

1 recipe Basic Vegetable Stock (page 56)

½ teaspoon hot pepper sauce
Salt

½ cup purchased basil pesto (optional)

1. Rinse beans. In a 3-quart soup pot combine beans and 8 cups cold water. Put the beans aside and let sit overnight. (This will make the beans less gaseous and cook faster when ready to cook.) Or you may combine the beans and 8 cups cold water. Bring to a boil. Reduce heat and simmer 2 minutes. Remove soup pot from heat. Let stand for 1 hour. Drain and rinse.

2. Drizzle oil in a 3-quart soup pot and swirl it around until the oil coats the entire surface of the bottom of the pan. Heat over high heat until hot. Add the celery, onion, fennel, pepper, parsley, bay leaves, and garlic. Stir around so that the vegetables cook evenly and the flavors mingle. When the vegetables just begin to turn brown, stir in the drained beans, the Basic Vegetable Stock, and the hot pepper sauce. Bring to a boil. Reduce heat to simmering and cook, covered, for 1½ hours, stirring occasionally to make sure there are no beans sticking to the bottom.

3. Check the beans to see if they are fully cooked. They should be firm with no hard core. If so, the beans are done. Season to taste with salt. (You should never season beans with salt before or during cooking because doing so will make the beans tough.) If desired, season with a little more pepper. Remove parsley sprigs and bay leaves.

4. Check the soup for consistency. If soup is too thick, add a little water. (The soup will thicken as it stands.) If you like, top each serving with a small spoonful of pesto.

Makes: 6 servings
Nutrition Facts per serving: 335 cal., 6 g total fat (1g sat. fat),
1 mg chol., 817 mg sodium, 53 g carbo., 21 g fiber, 17 g pro.
Daily Values: 13% vit. A, 13% vit. C, 13% calcium, 24% iron

**hite Bean Minestrone**

My version of a traditional Italian vegetable soup offers the great healthful combo of beans and pasta. Kids who won't touch a vegetable dig into this soup with gusto—maybe they don't know it's vegetable soup. It's even better the day after you make it.

2 tablespoons extra-virgin olive oil or canola oil

1 teaspoon dried oregano, crushed

1 teaspoon fennel seeds, crushed

4 stalks celery, chopped

1 medium carrot, chopped

1 onion, chopped

1 leek (white part only), halved lengthwise and cut ½ inch thick

1 tablespoon tomato paste

6 cloves garlic, minced

4 cups Basic Vegetable Stock (page 56) or water

2 14-ounce cans crushed organic plum tomatoes, undrained

1 14-ounce can organic cannellini or white kidney beans, drained and rinsed

2 tablespoons red wine vinegar

Bouquet Garni 2 (page 61)

½ cup green beans, cut into 1-inch pieces

½ cup cooked elbow macaroni

2 tablespoons balsamic vinegar

2 teaspoons salt

1. In a 3-quart soup pot heat the oil over medium heat for 1 minute. Add oregano and fennel seeds. Cook and stir until fragrant, about 15 seconds. Add celery, carrot, onion, leek, tomato paste, and garlic. Cook and stir for 5 minutes.

2. Add the Basic Vegetable Stock or water, undrained tomatoes, cannellini beans, red wine vinegar, and Bouquet Garni 2. Bring to a boil. Reduce heat to simmering and cook, covered, for 30 minutes. Add the green beans, cooked macaroni, balsamic vinegar, and salt. Cook 5 minutes more. Season to taste with black pepper.

Makes: 4 to 6 servings
Nutrition Facts per serving: 282 cal., 9 g total fat (1 g sat. fat),
0 mg chol., 1,717 mg sodium, 48 g carbo., 10 g fiber, 13 g pro.
Daily Values: 108% vit. A, 64% vit. C, 15% calcium, 21% iron

well-bread sandwiches

Don't underestimate what kids will eat! Sophisticated, exotic Summer Rolls are devoured at Calhoun. Sandwiches don't always have to mean "meat and bread." Wrap up kid-friendly fillings in rice paper, tortillas, or Indian bread.

Tuna Salad with Sprouts and Cucumbers on Kaiser Rolls

Wake up ho-hum tuna with a little Dijon mustard and white wine vinegar. I like to jazz it up even more by serving it on seeded sourdough rolls with fennel, sesame, and onion seeds. Bean sprouts and cucumbers add a refreshing crunch.

3   6-ounce cans solid white tuna (water pack), drained and broken into chunks

2   stalks celery, chopped

¼   cup chopped shallot

¼   cup mayonnaise

2   tablespoons Dijon mustard

1   tablespoon white wine vinegar

1   teaspoon salt

½   teaspoon black pepper

6   kaiser rolls, split

1   small cucumber, thinly sliced

1   cup alfalfa or clover sprouts

1. In a bowl combine tuna, celery, shallot, mayonnaise, mustard, vinegar, salt, and pepper. Spoon tuna mixture onto bottoms of rolls. Top with cucumber, sprouts, and roll tops.

Makes: 6 sandwiches

Nutrition Facts per half sandwich: 172 cal., 5 g total fat (I g sat. fat), 21 mg chol., 620 mg sodium, 18 g carbo., I g fiber, 14 g pro.
Daily Values: 3% vit. A, 4% vit. C, 5% calcium, 9% iron

Pan Bagnat

Here's all the summer flavor of the South of France, where even the humblest vegetable gets star treatment in the kitchen. In this recipe, the technique of wrapping the sandwiches tightly in plastic wrap means flavors marry and sweet juices soak into the bread. You can't believe how good this is until you taste it.

2 18-inch loaves baguette-style French bread or unsliced Italian bread, halved lengthwise

2 cloves garlic, smashed

Extra-virgin olive oil or canola oil

Salt

Freshly ground black pepper

1 sweet or red onion, thinly sliced

4 tomatoes, thinly sliced

1 seedless cucumber, peeled and thinly sliced

1 red bell pepper, thinly sliced

1 green bell pepper, thinly sliced

4 teaspoons capers, drained

1 6-ounce can solid white tuna (water pack), drained and broken into chunks

1. Rub the cut sides of each baguette with garlic, then drizzle with about 1 tablespoon olive oil. Sprinkle with salt and pepper.

2. On the bottom of each baguette, pile on the onion, tomatoes, cucumber, and bell peppers. Sprinkle each with a few capers. Top with chunks of tuna. Add baguette tops, squish them down, and wrap tightly in plastic wrap. Let stand at least 30 minutes so the juices will be soaked up by the bread.

3. To serve, cut each baguette into 3 pieces.

Makes: 6 servings
Nutrition Facts per serving: 371 cal., 13 g total fat (2 g sat. fat), 13 mg chol., 691 mg sodium, 49 g carbo., 5 g fiber, 16 g pro.
Daily Values: 38% vit. A, 126% vit. C, 8% calcium, 17% iron

Curried Chicken Salad Wraps

Looking for a way to repurpose leftover cooked chicken or turkey? Toss it with a sprightly curry sauce, tuck it into a whole wheat wrap, and no one will be the wiser. If you're lacking leftovers, prepare chicken breasts as directed in the recipe.

4 boneless, skinless chicken breast halves

1 tablespoon vegetable oil

2 tablespoons Dijon mustard

2 tablespoons light mayonnaise dressing

2 tablespoons light sour cream

2 tablespoons honey

2 teaspoons curry powder

2 teaspoons white wine vinegar

1 teaspoon salt

½ teaspoon ground cinnamon

½ teaspoon black pepper

½ cup dried cranberries or raisins

½ cup chopped almonds, toasted

½ cup sliced scallions

6 10-inch whole wheat tortillas

2 cups baby spinach

1. Preheat oven to 350°F. Rub the chicken breasts with the oil, then season both sides with a little salt and pepper. Place in a shallow baking pan and bake for 15 to 20 minutes or until no longer pink in the center. Set chicken aside to cool.

2. For curry sauce, in a small bowl combine the mustard, mayonnaise dressing, sour cream, honey, curry powder, vinegar, salt, cinnamon, and pepper. Set aside.

3. Cut the chicken breasts into thin strips. In a medium bowl combine the chicken, cranberries, almonds, and scallions.

4. Add the curry sauce to the chicken mixture and mix well. Place about ¾ cup of the chicken mixture on each tortilla, then top with some of the spinach. Roll up and halve crosswise.

Makes: 6 wraps
Nutrition Facts per half wrap: 234 cal., 8 g total fat (1 g sat. fat), 29 mg chol., 562 mg sodium, 27 g carbo., 3 g fiber, 16 g pro.
Daily Values: 7% vit. A, 5% vit. C, 5% calcium, 11% iron

If sandwiches have become ho-hum in your home, branch out a little. Package your kids' favorite sandwich "insides" in something new, like whole wheat tortillas or pita bread. Or add a surprising new flavor with a fresh herb or a new green, such as arugula, watercress, or spinach.

C hicken Caesar Wraps

A wonderful approach to a Caesar dressing gets rolled up in a whole wheat wrap. We omit the traditional raw egg and anchovy but maintain all the taste and satisfaction. For a slightly different twist on this classic, try smoked turkey in place of the chicken breast.

¾ **pound cooked chicken breast, cut into thin strips**

3 **cups chopped romaine**

¼ **cup shredded Parmesan cheese**

1 **recipe Caesar Dressing**

6 **10-inch whole wheat tortillas**

1. In a large bowl combine chicken, romaine, and Parmesan cheese. Add enough Caesar Dressing to coat all the ingredients (you may not need all of the dressing).

2. Divide the chicken mixture among the tortillas. Roll up and halve crosswise.

Caesar Dressing:
In a bowl combine ¼ cup sherry vinegar, ¼ cup extra-virgin olive oil or canola oil, 2 tablespoons grated Parmesan cheese, 2 tablespoons Dijon mustard, 1 tablespoon Worcestershire sauce, ½ teaspoon salt, ½ teaspoon black pepper, and 3 cloves garlic, halved. Blend together with an immersion blender.

Makes: 6 wraps
Nutrition Facts per half wrap: 219 cal., 8 g total fat (3 g sat. fat),
33 mg chol., 573 mg sodium, 20 g carbo., 2 g fiber, 17 g pro.
Daily Values: 9% vit. A, 6% vit. C, 17% calcium, 8% iron

moked Turkey and Swiss Cheese Po' Boys

This is how we translate a "hero sandwich" in New Orleans dialect and cuisine. Kids love this filling sandwich. Of course, they all think the name is great. You can substitute chicken, shrimp, or—to make it more authentic—fried oysters.

Light mayonnaise dressing

2 18-inch loaves whole wheat baguette-style French bread or unsliced French bread, halved lengthwise

Dijon mustard

1 pound thinly sliced smoked turkey

½ pound thinly sliced Swiss cheese

¼ head iceberg lettuce, shredded

2 Beefsteak tomatoes, thinly sliced

1 red or sweet onion, thinly sliced

Dill or bread-and-butter pickle chips

Hot pepper sauce

Salt and black pepper

1. Spread mayonnaise dressing on the cut side of each baguette bottom. Spread mustard on the cut side of each baguette top. On the bottom, pile on the turkey, cheese, lettuce, tomatoes, onion, and pickles. Sprinkle lightly with hot pepper sauce and season to taste with salt and pepper. Add tops, mustard side down.

2. To serve, cut each baguette into 3 pieces.

Makes: 6 servings
Nutrition Facts per serving: 480 cal., 17 g total fat (8 g sat. fat), 75 mg chol., 1,664 mg sodium, 48 g carbo., 4 g fiber, 33 g pro.
Daily Values: 16% vit. A, 22% vit. C, 43% calcium, 16% iron

Cheddar Cheese and Apple with Watercress

A rustic, hearty vegetarian sandwich. Make it on a crusty baguette or sliced seven-grain bread. Toasting the cheddar over apple slices makes for mouthwatering flavor, at once sweet, tart, and tarragon-creamy.

Fresh lemon juice

2 Granny Smith apples, cored, and thinly sliced

2 loaves unsliced French bread, halved lengthwise and toasted

6 to 8 slices cheddar cheese

1 bunch watercress

1 recipe Tarragon Mayonnaise

1. Sprinkle a little lemon juice over the apple slices and toss them together. (The lemon juice will keep the apples from oxidizing and turning brown.)

2. Preheat the broiler. On the bottom half of each toasted bread loaf, pile on the sliced apples. Top with cheese. Broil until the cheese melts. Remove from broiler and top with watercress.

3. Spread some of the Tarragon Mayonnaise on the top half of each toasted bread loaf. Place on the sandwich, mayonnaise side down. To serve, cut each sandwich into 3 pieces.

Tarragon Mayonnaise:
Combine 1 cup light mayonnaise dressing and 1 teaspoon chopped fresh tarragon. Let stand for a few minutes to let the flavors develop.

Makes: 6 servings
Nutrition Facts per serving: 624 cal., 21 g total fat (8 g sat. fat), 36 mg chol., 1,218 mg sodium, 89 g carbo., 6 g fiber, 21 g pro.
Daily Values: 9% vit. A, 10% vit. C, 32% calcium, 23% iron

Tarragon has a distinct flavor. It's almost an acquired taste. Introduce the herb to your family in this sandwich—the flavor and texture combination is wonderful.

Avocado, Cheddar, and Watercress on Baguette

The star of this fresh, sunny sandwich is the sparkling Lime-Cilantro Vinaigrette. This sandwich was created by Chef Tomek, who loves experimenting with the zingy flavors and wonderful combinations of Asian fusion cuisine.

1 bunch watercress

1 recipe Lime-Cilantro Vinaigrette

2 Hass avocados, seeded, peeled, and sliced

2 18-inch loaves baguette-style French bread, halved lengthwise

6 slices sharp white or yellow cheddar cheese

1. Wash and pick the watercress. To pick the watercress, twist off the lower two-third of each stem and discard. Toss the watercress with some of the vinaigrette until lightly coated.

2. Brush the avocado slices with some of the Lime-Cilantro Vinaigrette to prevent them from browning. Brush cut sides of each baguette half with some of the Lime-Cilantro Vinaigrette. On the bottom half of each baguette, pile on the cheese, avocado slices, and watercress. Add baguette tops.

3. To serve, cut each baguette into 3 pieces.

Lime-Cilantro Vinaigrette:
In a bowl combine ½ cup olive oil, 3 tablespoons fresh lime juice, 2 tablespoons white wine vinegar, 2 tablespoons Dijon mustard, 2 tablespoons chopped fresh cilantro, ½ teaspoon salt, and ½ teaspoon black pepper. Blend together with an immersion blender.

Makes: 6 servings
Nutrition Facts per serving: 593 cal., 39 g total fat (10 g sat. fat),
30 mg chol., 956 mg sodium, 45 g carbo., 5 g fiber, 15 g pro.
Daily Values: 20% vit. A, 20% vit. C, 28% calcium, 16% iron

Goat Cheese, Tomato, and Arugula on Foccacia

A robust Italian treat with the sweet and salty zing of pureed olives offset with creamy goat cheese. Kids at Calhoun, even the youngest, like goat cheese when it's not too strong. Choose a mild one like Montrachet.

1   cup pitted kalamata olives

1   tablespoon extra-virgin olive oil or canola oil

1   12×12-inch piece foccacia

8   ounces soft goat cheese

1   large Beefsteak tomato, sliced

    Salt and black pepper

2   cups baby arugula

1. Combine the olives and olive oil in a food processor. Process until pureed.

2. Cut the foccacia into six 6×4-inch pieces, then split each piece in half.

3. Spread the pureed olives on the cut side of half the foccacia. Spread the goat cheese on the cut side of the remaining foccacia. Place tomato slices on top of goat cheese and season with salt and pepper. Place arugula on top of tomato slices. Top with remaining foccacia pieces, olive side down.

Makes: 6 sandwiches
Nutrition Facts per half sandwich: 147 cal., 8 g total fat (3 g sat. fat),
11 mg chol., 323 mg sodium, 15 g carbo., 1 g fiber, 6 g pro.
Daily Values: 4% vit. A, 5% vit. C, 9% calcium, 4% iron

Roasted Vegetables with Goat Cheese Spread

Roasted vegetables are great as a side dish and they're terrific in this sandwich. The trick is to roast them so they are fully cooked but still have some crunch. Avoid burning or cooking them until they wilt. The cheese and garlic puree adds a welcome creamy tartness.

1 zucchini, cut lengthwise into ¼-inch slices

1 yellow summer squash, cut lengthwise into ¼-inch slices

1 red onion, halved and cut into ½-inch slices

2 red bell peppers

2 tablespoons extra-virgin olive oil or canola oil

1 tablespoon balsamic vinegar

½ teaspoon dried oregano, crushed

½ teaspoon garlic powder

½ teaspoon salt

½ teaspoon black pepper

½ cup soft goat cheese

½ cup softened cream cheese

2 cloves garlic

12 slices hearty whole grain bread

1 cup mesclun greens or other salad greens

1. Preheat oven to 400°F. Place zucchini, summer squash, and onion in a large bowl. Cut bell peppers into quarters. Remove stems, seeds, and membranes. Add bell peppers to bowl with the other vegetables. In a small bowl combine the olive oil, vinegar, oregano, garlic powder, salt, and pepper. Pour over the vegetables and toss to coat evenly. Arrange the vegetables on a baking sheet and roast until the vegetables are browned at the edges, about 15 minutes. Remove from oven and let cool.

2. Meanwhile, in a food processor combine goat cheese, cream cheese, and garlic. Process until combined. Spread some of the goat cheese mixture on 6 of the bread slices. Pile the roasted vegetables on top of the cheese mixture. Top each with greens and remaining bread slices.

Makes: 6 sandwiches
Nutrition Facts per half sandwich: 202 cal., 9 g total fat (4 g sat. fat),
14 mg chol., 440 mg sodium, 26 g carbo., 4 g fiber, 6 g pro.
Daily Values: 28% vit. A, 70% vit. C, 5% calcium, 9% iron

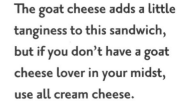

The goat cheese adds a little tanginess to this sandwich, but if you don't have a goat cheese lover in your midst, use all cream cheese.

# Egg White Frittata on Croissants

A nice option for lunch, this luscious frittata is big on good-for-you attributes: egg whites, little fat, and fresh veggies. Because it's served on flaky croissants, kids at Calhoun think this is like having an omelette sandwich.

8 **egg whites**

2 **egg yolks**

 Salt and black pepper

2 **tablespoons olive oil**

½ **red or sweet onion, thinly sliced**

1 **red bell pepper, thinly sliced**

¼ **cup finely chopped fresh parsley**

¼ **cup shredded cheddar cheese or Swiss cheese**

6 **croissants, split**

 Dijon mustard

1. Preheat oven to 375°F.

2. Beat the egg whites and egg yolks together until foamy. Add salt and pepper to taste.

3. Drizzle the olive oil in a large ovenproof skillet and swirl it around until the oil coats the entire surface. Heat over high heat until hot. Add the onion and bell pepper. Cook and stir until they just begin to caramelize and turn a little bit brown.

4. Add the egg mixture to skillet. Reduce heat to medium. Stir the eggs with the onion and bell pepper until combined. Stir in the parsley and cheese.

5. Allow the eggs to cook slowly over medium heat until you see they are beginning to brown on the bottom when you raise them with a spatula. Transfer skillet to the oven and bake for 8 to 10 minutes or until slightly puffed and a knife inserted in the center comes out clean.

6. Remove frittata from oven and let cool for 10 minutes (frittata will continue to cook). Turn frittata out onto a large plate and cut into 6 pieces. Spread the cut sides of each croissant with Dijon mustard. Place 1 frittata piece on each croissant. This is as good cold as it is warm.

Makes: 6 servings

Nutrition Facts per serving: 355 cal., 20 g total fat (9 g sat. fat),
115 mg chol., 789 mg sodium, 29 g carbo., 2 g fiber, 12 g pro.
Daily Values: 37% vit. A, 70% vit. C, 8% calcium, 9% iron

# Eggless Egg Salad on White Bread

There's nothing bland about the ingredients in this great sandwich that takes just a few minutes to toss together. Even though it's made with tofu, a lot of the kids will insist it's egg salad—even after you tell them otherwise!

1	8-ounce package extra-firm tofu, drained
4	stalks celery, finely chopped
2	tablespoons finely chopped shallot
1	tablespoon Dijon mustard
1	tablespoon white wine vinegar
½	teaspoon paprika
½	teaspoon ground turmeric
12	slices white bread
6	iceberg lettuce leaves

1. Break the tofu into small, crumbly pieces. In a bowl combine tofu, celery, shallot, Dijon mustard, vinegar, paprika, and turmeric. Spread the salad on 6 pieces of the bread. Top each with a lettuce leaf and the remaining bread.

Makes: 6 sandwiches
Nutrition Facts per half sandwich: 87 cal., 2 g total fat (0 g sat. fat),
1 mg chol., 189 mg sodium, 15 g carbo., 1 g fiber, 4 g pro.
Daily Values: 3% vit. A, 4% vit. C, 5% calcium, 7% iron

Marinated Sesame Tofu on Ciabatta

Forget thinking that tofu lacks taste. In this recipe, it's marinated overnight to soak up the most intensely delicious flavor and then roasted until it's a glossy, golden brown. The dense, rustic ciabatta bread provides a chewy contrast.

¼ **cup soy sauce**

¼ **cup sherry vinegar**

¼ **cup vegetable oil**

¼ **cup toasted sesame oil**

¼ **cup Dijon mustard**

1 **8-ounce package extra-firm tofu, drained**

2 **tablespoons sesame seeds**

2 **loaves ciabatta bread**

1 **seedless cucumber, thinly sliced**

2 **cups arugula**

1. Whisk together the soy sauce, vinegar, vegetable oil, sesame oil, and Dijon mustard. Set aside.

2. Cut tofu into ¼-inch-thick slices. Place in a shallow dish in a single layer. Pour the soy sauce mixture over the tofu. Cover with plastic wrap and let marinate overnight.

3. Preheat oven to 400°F. Remove the tofu from the marinade, reserving the marinade. Place tofu on a baking sheet and sprinkle with sesame seeds. Bake until the tofu is browned, about 15 minutes. Remove from oven and let cool.

4. Cut the ciabatta into 6 pieces; cut each piece in half horizontally. Whisk the marinade again to emulsify it. Brush some of the marinade on the cut sides of the bread. Divide the cucumber slices among the bread bottoms. Layer with tofu and arugula. Add bread tops.

Makes: 6 servings
Nutrition Facts per serving: 179 cal., 11 g total fat (2 g sat. fat),
0 mg chol., 379 mg sodium, 15 g carbo., 2 g fiber, 8 g pro.
Daily Values: 5% vit. A, 6% vit. C, 9% calcium, 8% iron

I love that some of our older students have really developed a passion for cooking and eating good food. When they began to save their money for good quality kitchen tools, I knew they were hooked!

 ortobello Cheeseburgers

Better than any veggie burger and as tasty as a burger made from meat. You'll experience a rich smoky flavor and nice juicy texture when you bite into these mushroom caps. It's a win, win—you get all of the satisfaction of eating a cheeseburger without the guilt.

1 tablespoon olive oil

6 large portobello mushroom caps

6 cheddar or American cheese slices

6 hamburger buns, split and toasted

6 sweet onion slices

6 Beefsteak tomato slices

6 lettuce leaves

Mustard, light mayonnaise dressing, organic ketchup, pickle slices, or other condiments of your choice

1 recipe Oven French Fries (page 176) (optional)

1. Drizzle olive oil in a nonstick skillet and swirl it around until the oil coats the entire surface. Heat over high heat until hot.

2. Add the mushrooms to the skillet with their tops down. Weight them down with a bacon press or a small skillet. Reduce heat to medium. After about 5 minutes, remove the bacon press or skillet providing the weight and turn the mushrooms so the tops are up. Top each mushroom with a slice of cheese. Cook another 5 minutes. Remove skillet from heat.

3. Serve mushrooms on buns. Top with onion, tomato, and lettuce. Add additional condiments and serve with Oven French Fries, if you like.

Makes: 6 servings
Nutrition Facts per serving: 317 cal., 17 g total fat (6 g sat. fat), 33 mg chol., 780 mg sodium, 33 g carbo., 3 g fiber, 15 g pro.
Daily Values: 22% vit. A, 19% vit. C, 30% calcium, 16% iron

oasted Portobello Mushrooms and Red Peppers on Focaccia

Two kinds of peppers contribute to this vibrant sandwich: Sweet red peppers in a balsamic marinade contrast with a smoky chipotle pepper mayonnaise. Italian, Latin, delicious. If you like, give it a French accent by adding soft goat cheese.

2   red bell peppers

6   large portobello mushroom caps

2   tablespoons extra-virgin olive oil or canola oil

1   tablespoon balsamic vinegar

½   teaspoon salt

½   teaspoon black pepper

⅓   cup mayonnaise

2   to 3 canned chipotle chile peppers in adobo sauce*

1   clove garlic

6   focaccia rolls, split

1   cup baby arugula

1. Cut bell peppers into quarters. Remove stems, seeds, and membranes. Place bell peppers and mushroom caps in a bowl. Combine oil, vinegar, salt, and pepper. Pour over vegetables and toss to coat.

2. Preheat oven to 375°F. Arrange vegetables on a baking sheet and roast until the mushrooms are soft and cooked all the way through, about 15 minutes. Remove vegetables from oven and let cool.

3. In a food processor combine mayonnaise, chipotle peppers, and garlic. Process until combined. (Use fewer chipotle peppers for a less spicy mayonnaise.)

4. Spread the mayonnaise mixture on the cut sides of each focaccia roll. Place 1 mushroom cap on the bottom half of each roll. Layer with bell peppers and arugula. Add roll tops.

***Note:** Chipotle chile peppers in adobo sauce are sold in the Hispanic foods section of your local market. Be careful! They can be very hot!

Makes: 6 servings
Nutrition Facts per serving: 270 cal., 14 g total fat (2 g sat. fat),
10 mg chol., 345 mg sodium, 34 g carbo., 3 g fiber, 9 g pro.
Daily Values: 48% vit. A, 127% vit. C, 11% calcium, 8% iron

Grilled Cheese Sandwiches with Tomato

The problem with making this sandwich at Calhoun is that when we serve it, kids pass by everything else in the lunch line. One day, we made a double mistake that guaranteed no one would ask for a hot entrée. We offered grilled cheese along with another favorite: chicken soup. At least we know better than to serve grilled cheese on a day when we're also offering fish!

2   tablespoons safflower or canola oil

1   tablespoon butter or soy margarine

12 slices hearty whole grain bread

6   slices American cheese

2   large Beefsteak tomatoes, thinly sliced

1. In a small saucepan combine the safflower oil and butter. Heat until butter melts.

2. Spread oil mixture on 1 side of each slice of bread. With oiled sides down, top 6 slices of bread with cheese and tomato. Top with remaining bread slices, oiled sides up.

3. Preheat a large nonstick skillet or griddle over medium heat. Place as many sandwiches as will fit in the hot skillet and cook until toasted. (When you check them with a spatula, they should be golden brown.) At this point, flip the sandwiches with the spatula. (If you have a bacon press or a small skillet, you can place it on top of the sandwiches and it will press the bread and the cheese together.) When the second side of the sandwiches is toasted, transfer to a warm plate. Repeat with any remaining sandwiches.

Makes: 6 sandwiches
Nutrition Facts per sandwich half: 204 cal., 11 g total fat (4 g sat. fat), 17 mg chol., 510 mg sodium, 23 g carbo., 3 g fiber, 7 g pro.
Daily Values: 6% vit. A, 5% vit. C, 11% calcium, 7% iron

Occasionally we do serve what many consider to be 100-percent kid food. You can't omit a beloved favorite like grilled cheese.

Vegetarian Summer Rolls

Nobody was more surprised than I the first time these rolls appeared on the lunch menu and the kids went crazy for them. I remember saying to Chef Tomek, who created them, "The kids will never eat these." But the kids go wild over them and we get many requests for second helpings. I love them too and put them on the menu so often that the chefs say, "Not again!"

1	seedless cucumber
12	10-inch round rice papers*
1	bunch fresh basil
1	bunch fresh mint
1½	cups cold cooked rice
1½	cups shredded carrot
1½	cups shredded daikon**
2	cups hoisin sauce

1. Quarter the cucumber lengthwise, then cut each quarter into 3 long pieces. Trim to 4-inch lengths.

2. Fill a bowl with very hot water and lay out a large cotton towel or napkin that has been sprinkled with water. Place 1 rice paper in the hot water and let it soften for 15 seconds or so, until it is flexible and nearly transparent. Lay it on the towel. Working in the center of the rice paper, place 2 basil leaves and 2 mint leaves, then top with 2 tablespoons of rice, pressing down slightly. Add about 1 tablespoon shredded carrot, 1 tablespoon shredded daikon, and 1 piece of cucumber. Top with 1 tablespoon hoisin sauce.

3. To wrap the summer roll, fold 2 sides of rice paper over filling, then roll into an egg roll shape. Serve the remaining hoisin sauce on the side for dipping.

***Note:** Rice papers can be found at Asian groceries or specialty food stores. They are about 10 inches in diameter and are translucent, papery, and made from rice flour. In order to use the rice papers, they need to be soaked in hot water, but don't leave them soaking in the water for too long or they get gummy. They are very sticky and need to be placed on cotton towels that have been sprinkled lightly with water.

****Note:** Daikon is a long white Asian radish.

Makes: 12 summer rolls
Nutrition Facts per roll: 114 cal., 1 g total fat (0 g sat. fat), 0 mg chol., 193 mg sodium, 24 g carbo., 2 g fiber, 2 g pro.
Daily Values: 90% vit. A, 19% vit. C, 3% calcium, 9% iron

 egetable Quesadillas

Toasted tortillas layered with cheese and vegetables are meltingly good. We sometimes serve these at school, sliced into sections, as afternoon snacks. You can top them with salsa if you want to add another layer of flavor.

8 fresh button mushrooms, sliced

2 small zucchini, chopped

1 head broccoli, chopped

1 red bell pepper, chopped

1 medium carrot, shredded

1 red onion, thinly sliced

8 8-inch flour tortillas

1 cup shredded sharp cheddar cheese

1 cup shredded Monterey Jack cheese

Salt and black pepper

1. Line a large baking sheet with aluminum foil.

2. Place a steamer basket in a saucepan. Place mushrooms, zucchini, broccoli, bell pepper, carrot, and onion in steamer basket over 1 inch of boiling water. Steam, covered, until vegetables are tender but still firm, 2 to 6 minutes. Remove basket and discard liquid.

3. Preheat broiler. Place 4 tortillas, side by side, on the prepared baking sheet. On each tortilla layer cheddar cheese, steamed vegetables, then Monterey Jack cheese. Season to taste with salt and pepper. Top each with another tortilla.

4. Broil until tortillas are lightly browned. Carefully turn tortillas over and broil on the other side until lightly browned.

5. Remove quesadillas from the baking sheet and let cool for 5 minutes. Cut into quarters.

Makes: 4 quesadillas

Nutrition Facts per half quesadilla: 228 cal., 12 g total fat (7 g sat. fat),
28 mg chol., 314 mg sodium, 21 g carbo., 3 g fiber, 11 g pro.
Daily Values: 72% vit. A, 90% vit. C, 27% calcium, 10% iron

Vegetable Fajitas

These are so tasty and so satisfying—the vegetables stir-fry with a minimum of effort. Lime juice adds a shock of citrus and the smooth guacamole (page 48) rounds it out.

1 zucchini, cut into thin strips about 2 inches long

1 yellow summer squash, cut into thin strips about 2 inches long

1 onion, thinly sliced

1 red bell pepper, thinly sliced

1 teaspoon ground cumin

1 teaspoon finely ground sea salt

½ teaspoon chili powder

½ teaspoon black pepper

1 clove garlic, minced

2 teaspoons safflower or canola oil

½ teaspoon fresh lime juice

1 recipe Chef Bobo's Simple and Delicious Guacamole (see page 48)

6 8-inch flour tortillas

Light sour cream

1. In a bowl combine zucchini, summer squash, onion, bell pepper, cumin, sea salt, chili powder, black pepper, and garlic. Drizzle with oil. Toss to combine.

2. Heat a large nonstick skillet over high heat until hot. Add vegetables to skillet and cook and stir until crisp-tender. Remove skillet from heat. Sprinkle lime juice over the vegetables and stir it in.

3. Spread some Simple and Delicious Guacamole on each tortilla. Top with vegetables and a little sour cream. Roll up tortillas.

Makes: 6 servings
Nutrition Facts per serving: 229 cal., 13 g total fat (3 g sat. fat), 7 mg chol., 420 mg sodium, 24 g carbo., 4 g fiber, 5 g pro.
Daily Values: 37% vit. A, 83% vit. C, 10% calcium, 11% iron

Kids think wraps are great, so take advantage of the love affair and tuck in perfectly seasoned, crisp-tender vegetables.

Hummus Pitas with Cucumber-Yogurt Sauce

This is so refreshing—a Middle Eastern taste treat that appeals to vegetarians and nonvegetarians alike. I love the tangy hummus combined with a cucumber-flecked yogurt sauce. The kids at Calhoun prefer it on pita bread.

2 cups whole milk yogurt

1 cucumber, very finely chopped

¼ cup tahini (sesame seed paste)

½ teaspoon salt

6 pita bread rounds, halved crosswise

1 recipe Hummus

2 plum tomatoes, thinly sliced

2 cups shredded romaine

1. For Cucumber-Yogurt Sauce, in a bowl combine yogurt, cucumber, tahini, and salt. Set aside.

2. Preheat oven to 350°F. Wrap pitas tightly in foil and place in oven for a few minutes to warm. Fill each pita with Hummus, 2 tablespoons of the sauce, tomatoes, and romaine. Serve remaining sauce on the side.

Hummus:
In a food processor combine two 14-ounce cans garbanzo beans, drained; ¼ cup olive oil; ¼ cup tahini (sesame seed paste); 3 tablespoons fresh lemon juice; 1 tablespoon toasted sesame oil; ½ teaspoon ground cumin; and 2 cloves garlic. Process until smooth. If too thick, add some water until the hummus is the consistency of soft mashed potatoes.

Makes: 12 pita halves
Nutrition Facts per pita half: 293 cal., 14 g total fat (2 g sat. fat), 5 mg chol., 505 mg sodium, 34 g carbo., 5 g fiber, 10 g pro.
Daily Values: 9% vit. A, 20% vit. C, 12% calcium, 12% iron

BLT Wrap

Not surprisingly, this is one of the most popular sandwiches at Calhoun. I make it with hearty whole wheat wraps instead of white toast. The real secret to my version (don't tell the kids) is how little bacon it takes to completely satisfy your desire for a true BLT. The kids never complain that there's not enough bacon in it. They do complain when we run out!

1	heart romaine
6	8-inch whole wheat flour tortillas
	Light mayonnaise dressing
2	large Beefsteak tomatoes,* chopped
6	slices thick bacon, cooked until crisp

1. Prepare romaine by breaking all the leaves apart and washing under cold running water. Dry romaine and tear it into bite-size pieces.

2. Spread 1 side of each tortilla with mayonnaise dressing. Top each with a handful of the lettuce, followed by chopped tomatoes. Crumble bacon and sprinkle over the lettuce and tomatoes. Roll up and halve crosswise.

*__Note:__ Beefsteak tomatoes are known for their juiciness and flavor. They're wonderful raw or cooked.

Makes: 6 wraps

Nutrition Facts per wrap: 235 cal., 10 g total fat (3 g sat. fat), 10 mg chol., 598 mg sodium, 31 g carbo., 3 g fiber, 7 g pro.
Daily Values: 20% vit. A, 28% vit. C, 3% calcium, 10% iron

the dinner bell bobo

Tempt your kids with adventuresome choices, woo them with fabulous tastes, wow them with bold seasonings, dazzle them with invigorating herbs and sublime spices, and heap on the flavor.

Beef Curry

We don't serve much beef at school, but when we serve this we try to make enough for seconds! Its heritage is Asian, although it's anything but traditional—just a great new way of combining the exotic with the familiar and ratcheting up the flavors. If you like, serve a little of the Cilantro, Tomato, Cucmber, and Yogurt Raita (page 20) on the side.

1 **pound beef flank steak**

1 **large red bell pepper, coarsely chopped**

1 **medium onion, coarsely chopped**

½ **teaspoon chili powder**

2 **cloves garlic, halved**

6 **tablespoons vegetable oil**

2 **tablespoons soy sauce**

1 **cup unsweetened coconut milk**

½ **cup fresh basil leaves, chopped**

½ **cup fresh mint leaves, chopped**

1 **tablespoon lime zest**

½ **teaspoon salt**

1 **recipe Simple Steamed Rice (page 168)**

1. Slice the steak across the grain into very thin pieces. Set aside.

2. In a blender container combine the bell pepper, onion, chili powder, and garlic. Blend until pureed. (If necessary, add a tablespoon or 2 of water to the blender.)

3. Heat oil in a skillet over medium heat until hot. Stir in the pureed mixture. Cook and stir until dark. Add the beef pieces and the soy sauce. Cook for 2 minutes, stirring the beef around constantly.

4. Stir in the coconut milk, basil, mint, lime zest, and salt. Heat through. Serve over rice.

Makes: 6 servings
Nutrition Facts per serving with steamed rice: 435 cal., 30 g total fat (11 g sat. fat), 40 mg chol., 549 mg sodium, 20 g carbo., 1 g fiber, 19 g pro.
Daily Values: 32% vit. A, 82% vit. C, 3% calcium, 25% iron

Ground Sirloin with Garlic and Shallot Butter

I've been making this for 25 years. It's elegant and easy. The Worcestershire sauce and Dijon mustard keep it from being "hamburger-esque." Substitute turkey for the sirloin, if you want—just make sure the turkey isn't rare. It should be 165°F when tested with a thermometer.

2	tablespoons Dijon mustard
1	teaspoon Worcestershire sauce
½	teaspoon black pepper
	Salt
1 ½	pounds ground sirloin
¼	cup dry red wine
3	tablespoons finely chopped shallot or onion
1	teaspoon chopped fresh thyme
1	teaspoon minced garlic
2	tablespoons butter or soy margarine

1. In a bowl combine mustard, Worcestershire sauce, and pepper. Season to taste with salt. Add ground sirloin. Mix well. Divide meat mixture into 4 equal portions. Shape each portion into a patty. Set aside.

2. In a small saucepan combine wine, shallot or onion, thyme, and garlic. Cook until wine is almost evaporated, about 3 minutes. Cool slightly. Add butter, stirring until combined. Keep butter mixture warm.

3. Cook patties in a skillet over medium heat about 12 minutes for medium-rare or about 15 minutes for medium, turning once so both sides brown.

4. To serve, smear patties with butter mixture.

Makes: 4 servings

Nutrition Facts per serving: 318 cal., 14 g total fat (7 g sat. fat), 97 mg chol., 494 mg sodium, 3 g carbo., 0 g fiber, 38 g pro.
Daily Values: 7% vit. A, 2% vit. C, 2% calcium, 22% iron

Sweet-and-Sour Pork

I found this recipe in a long-forgotten cookbook in New Orleans about 30 years ago, and I've been making this marvelous dish ever since. No matter the origin, it's incredibly easy to prepare and you'll be stunned by the truly authentic Chinese flavor. Need I say how much kids love pineapple?

1 pound lean boneless pork, cut into bite-size chunks

1 teaspoon dry sherry

½ teaspoon salt

¼ teaspoon black pepper

3 tablespoons all-purpose flour

3 tablespoons cornstarch

½ cup safflower or canola oil

1 medium carrot, thinly sliced

⅔ cup bite-size seeded cucumber chunks

½ cup thinly sliced fresh mushrooms

1 clove garlic, minced

1 recipe Sweet-and-Sour Sauce

1. In a bowl combine the pork, dry sherry, salt, and pepper. Cover and let stand for 30 minutes. In another bowl stir together the flour and cornstarch. Remove pork from sherry mixture. Roll in flour mixture until well coated.

2. Heat oil in a large nonstick skillet over high heat until hot. Carefully fry the pork, a few chunks at a time, in the hot oil until lightly browned and slightly crisp. (Be careful not to crowd the pork or it will get gummy.) Remove pork from oil and drain on paper towels. Discard oil in skillet, reserving 1 tablespoon.

3. Return the skillet with the reserved 1 tablespoon oil to the heat. Add the carrot, cucumber, mushrooms, and garlic. Cook and stir for 1 minute. Remove vegetables from skillet and drain on paper towels.

4. Return pork and vegetables to skillet. Pour Sweet-and-Sour Sauce over the pork and vegetables, stirring to combine. Heat through over low heat.

Sweet-and-Sour Sauce:
In a 1-quart saucepan combine 1 cup fresh pineapple chunks, ¼ cup ketchup, ¼ cup cider vinegar, 2 tablespoons honey, 1 teaspoon soy sauce, and 1 teaspoon grated fresh ginger. Bring to a simmer over low heat. Combine 2 tablespoons cold water and 1 teaspoon cornstarch; stir into saucepan. Cook and stir until thick.

Makes: 4 servings
Nutrition Facts per serving: 357 cal., 13 g total fat (3 g sat. fat), 62 mg chol., 601 mg sodium, 32 g carbo., 2 g fiber, 27 g pro.
Daily Values: 81% vit. A, 17% vit. C, 4% calcium, 9% iron

For me and my staff, it's not just about feeding kids. It's about health and well-being. It's about teaching food as a life skill.

**P**an-Roasted Sage Pork Tenderloin

This is the most tender cut of pork, with little fat and loads of flavor. Two cautions: Be careful the pork doesn't dry out, and don't substitute dry sage; it's too brittle and will break if you try to wrap it around the pork.

1	1-pound pork tenderloin
1	tablespoon olive oil
12	fresh sage leaves
1	teaspoon kosher salt
1	teaspoon freshly ground black pepper
½	cup water
½	teaspoon fresh lemon juice

1. Preheat oven to 350°F. Brush tenderloin with oil. Wrap the sage leaves all along the length of the tenderloin. (They should stick easily to the surface.) Season with the salt and pepper.

2. Heat a nonstick ovenproof skillet over high heat until hot. Add the tenderloin. Cook until golden brown, 7 to 8 minutes. Turn frequently to brown on all sides. Transfer skillet to oven. Roast tenderloin until done (160°F), 10 to 20 minutes. Transfer tenderloin to a serving platter. Keep warm.

3. Add water to skillet. Boil over medium heat. Scrape up the browned bits with a wooden spoon. Let bubble until reduced by half. Stir in lemon juice. Serve with pork.

Makes: 4 servings
Nutrition Facts per serving: 166 cal., 7 g total fat (2 g sat. fat), 73 mg chol., 529 mg sodium, 1 g carbo., 0 g fiber, 24 g pro.
Daily Values: 1% vit. A, 2% vit. C, 2% calcium, 9% iron

Honey-Marinated Pork

These tender cubes of pork are best grilled but can be pan-roasted. The results will be similarly sweet, tangy, and tantalizing for a delightful marriage of Mediterranean and Asian cuisines.

½ **cup soy sauce**

½ **cup water**

¼ **cup honey**

2 **tablespoons red wine vinegar**

1 **tablespoon minced garlic**

1 **tablespoon chopped fresh sage**

1 **tablespoon grated fresh ginger**

1 **teaspoon paprika**

Salt

2 ½ **pounds lean boneless pork, cut into 2-inch cubes**

2 **tablespoons canola oil**

1 **tablespoon fresh lemon juice**

1 **tablespoon chopped fresh cilantro**

1. For marinade, in a bowl combine soy sauce, water, honey, vinegar, garlic, sage, ginger, and paprika. Season to taste with salt. Add pork cubes to marinade. Marinate in refrigerator for 1 to 24 hours.

2. Drain pork, reserving marinade. In a 12-inch nonstick skillet heat oil until hot. Add pork cubes. Cook the pork cubes until well browned and fully cooked, about 15 minutes.

3. Meanwhile, in a small saucepan combine ¼ cup of the reserved marinade, lemon juice, and cilantro. Bring to a boil. Serve over pork cubes.

To grill: Use wooden skewers that have been soaked in water for 30 minutes. Grill on one side for 10 minutes, then turn and grill on other side for another 5 minutes.

Makes: 8 servings

Nutrition Facts per serving: 248 cal., 8 g total fat (3 g sat. fat), 77 mg chol., 815 mg sodium, 8 g carbo., 0 g fiber, 33 g pro.

Daily Values: 5% vit. A, 4% vit. C, 5% calcium, 7% iron

Lamb Ragout and Pasta

I adapted this from a recipe a great Italian cook shared with me. It's a hearty one-dish meal that tastes even better if you make it a day ahead. Needless to say, make the pasta only when you're ready to serve it.

12 ounces dried penne pasta

2 tablespoons olive oil

½ cup finely chopped onion

1 pound ground lamb

½ cup dry white wine

1 tablespoon chopped
    fresh rosemary

2 cups canned
    organic tomatoes

    Salt

    Black pepper

    Grated Romano cheese

1. Cook pasta according to package directions. Drain.

2. Heat oil in a 3-quart soup pot over high heat until hot. Reduce heat. Add the onion. Cook and stir until tender but not brown. Add the ground lamb. Cook and stir until browned. Stir in the wine and rosemary. Simmer until the wine evaporates.

3. Meanwhile, pour the undrained tomatoes into a bowl and crush the tomatoes with your hands. Add the tomatoes to the soup pot. Bring to a boil. Reduce heat and simmer until the juices are pretty well evaporated and the ragout is thick, about 30 minutes. Season to taste with salt and pepper.

4. Serve ragout over pasta. Sprinkle with Romano cheese.

Makes: 6 servings
Nutrition Facts per serving: 518 cal., 17 g total fat (6 g sat. fat),
55 mg chol., 409 mg sodium, 62 g carbo., 3 g fiber, 25 g pro.
Daily Values: 10% vit. A, 20% vit. C, 10 calcium, 21% iron

We've known kids love pizza and pasta, but we've figured out how to get them to love curries, roasted caulifower, and chickpeas too.

Simple Lamb Curry

When we start preparing this lovely, fragrant curry at school, the aroma wafts up from the kitchen and a line forms outside the lunchroom long before lunch begins. This recipe is even better the day after when all the flavors have saturated the meat. Sweeten and enhance the taste with prepared mango chutney—available at most supermarkets.

2 pounds lamb stew meat, cubed

Salt and black pepper

½ cup all-purpose flour

3 tablespoons safflower or canola oil

3 small onions, thinly sliced

3 tablespoons curry powder

1 teaspoon grated fresh ginger

1 teaspoon cumin seeds

1 teaspoon cardamom seeds

½ teaspoon black pepper

2 cloves garlic, minced

3 cups water

Hot cooked rice

1 recipe Cilantro, Tomato, Cucumber, and Yogurt Raita (page 20)

1. Season the lamb cubes with salt and pepper. Coat lamb cubes with flour, shaking off any excess.

2. Heat 2 tablespoons of the oil in a 3- or 4-quart soup pot over high heat until hot. Add the lamb. Cook and stir until nicely browned on all sides. Remove lamb from pot. Set aside.

3. Add the remaining 1 tablespoon oil to the pot. Add onions, curry powder, ginger, cumin seeds, cardamom seeds, pepper, and garlic. Cook and stir until the spices are very fragrant, about 30 seconds. Add water to pot. Stir in lamb cubes.

4. Bring to a boil. Reduce heat and simmer until lamb is very tender, about 1 to 1½ hours. Season to taste with additional salt and pepper. Serve over rice with Raita.

Makes: 6 servings

Nutrition Facts per serving with rice: 487 cal., 16 g total fat (3 g sat. fat), 98 mg chol.,624 mg sodium, 47 g carbo., 2 g fiber, 36 g pro.
Daily Values: 1% vit. A, 2% vit. C, 5% calcium, 36% iron

# Whole Roasted Chicken

You know how cooks say they have the best roast chicken recipe ever? Well, I do. Foolproof and flavorful, the chicken comes out juicy and crisp every time. The secret is browning the chicken before you roast it, which is how you learn to make roasted chicken at culinary school.

1 **3- to 3½-pound chicken**
   Kosher salt
   Freshly ground black pepper
3 **sprigs fresh rosemary**
3 **sprigs fresh thyme**
1 **head garlic, unpeeled and halved**
1 **tablespoon olive oil**

1. Preheat oven to 350°F.

2. Wash the chicken, inside and out, under cold running water. Be sure to pat it completely dry inside as well as outside with paper towels. Cut off the end tips of the wings.

3. Generously season the inside and outside of the chicken with salt and pepper. Place the rosemary, thyme, and garlic inside the chicken.

4. Truss the chicken by tying the legs together at the base of the drumsticks with a piece of string. Bring another piece of string around the front over the breast, turn the chicken over and tie it in the back with the wings held close to the body.

5. Heat oil in a sauté pan over high heat until hot. Place the trussed chicken in the hot oil on its side. Brown for 7 minutes. With a meat fork or tongs, turn the chicken to brown on the opposite side for another 7 minutes.

6. Lay the chicken on its back and roast about 50 minutes. The chicken is done when the thigh juices run clear and a leg is easily moved. Let stand for 15 minutes before carving.

7. Meanwhile, pour off the excess fat and discard it. Add ¼ cup water to the sauté pan. Boil over medium heat. Scrape up the browned bits with a wooden spoon. Let it bubble and thicken. Spoon over chicken.

Makes: 6 servings
Nutrition Facts per serving: 234 cal., 14 g total fat (4 g sat. fat),
79 mg chol., 234 mg sodium, 0 g carbo., 0 g fiber, 24 g pro.
Daily Values: 1% calcium, 6% iron

Fried Chicken

The question I'm most often asked? "Chef Bobo, when are we going to have fried chicken?" The key to this recipe is the perfect mix of seasonings for taste and a buttermilk marinade for tenderizing. Don't count on leftovers!

1	2- to 3-pound chicken fryer, cut into 10 pieces
4	cups buttermilk
2	tablespoons fine sea salt
2	tablespoons black pepper
1	tablespoon hot pepper sauce
3	cloves garlic, smashed
2	cups all-purpose flour
1	teaspoon garlic powder
1	teaspoon dry mustard
1	teaspoon paprika
½	teaspoon chili powder
¼	teaspoon ground cumin
	Canola or safflower oil

1. Wash chicken. Pat dry with paper towels. For marinade, combine buttermilk, 1 tablespoon of the salt, 1 tablespoon of the pepper, hot pepper sauce, and garlic. Place chicken in a large container. Pour marinade over chicken. Cover and marinate in refrigerator for 24 hours.

2. In a shallow dish combine flour, the remaining 1 tablespoon salt, the remaining 1 tablespoon pepper, garlic powder, mustard, paprika, chili powder, and cumin. Take a pinch of the flour mixture and taste it—it should be a bit salty and peppery.

3. Drain chicken but do not wipe off. Coat the chicken pieces with the flour mixture. Preheat oven to 350°F. Place a cooling rack in a large baking sheet or jelly roll pan. Set aside.

4. Pour oil into a deep, heavy pot. The oil should not reach more than halfway up the side of the pot. Heat over high heat to 350°F. Reduce heat to medium. Place the chicken, one piece at a time, in the hot oil. (Be very careful, as the oil will boil up and you don't want it to overflow.) Fry chicken, 3 or 4 pieces at a time, until golden brown. Remove chicken from oil and place on cooling rack.

5. Once all the chicken has been fried, transfer the baking sheet or jelly roll pan holding the cooling rack to the oven. (This will help crisp the batter on the chicken and let much of the oil drain from the chicken.) Bake until fully cooked (180°F), about 20 minutes.

Makes: 6 servings
Nutrition Facts per serving: 165 cal., 17 g total fat (3 g sat. fat), 53 mg chol., 391 mg sodium, 8 g carbo., 0 g fiber, 18 g pro.
Daily Values: 1% vit. A, 1% vit. C, 3% calcium, 8% iron

At times, I admit, I feel less like a classically trained chef and more like a fantastic amalgam of chef, teacher, diplomat, salesman, negotiator, cheerleader, and child psychologist.

Pan-Crisped Chicken

Here's a pan-roasting technique that results in a crisp, succulent chicken bursting with flavor. It's as crisp as Peking duck, even if you want to prepare it without the skin. Rustic, simple, and sensational.

1 **2 ½- to 3-pound chicken, cut into 10 pieces**

4 **tablespoons extra-virgin olive oil or canola oil**

2 **tablespoons fresh lemon juice**

1 **sprig fresh rosemary, needles stripped from stem**

¼ **teaspoon fine sea salt**

⅛ **teaspoon black pepper**

1 **clove garlic, halved**

½ **cup water**

1. Wash chicken. Pat dry with paper towels. Remove skin from chicken pieces.

2. In a blender container combine 2 tablespoons of the oil, 1 tablespoon of the lemon juice, rosemary, salt, pepper, and garlic. Blend until pureed. Rub the puree onto the chicken pieces. Marinate in refrigerator for 2 hours.

3. Heat the remaining 2 tablespoons oil in a skillet over high heat. Add the chicken pieces, skin sides down, to the skillet. Reduce heat to medium-high. Cook 1 minute to lightly sear the chicken. Turn chicken pieces skin sides up. Set another skillet directly on top of the cooking chicken pieces to weight them down.

4. Cook chicken, turning pieces again after about 7 or 8 minutes. Return the skillet providing the weight after each turning. Chicken pieces will probably need to be turned 3 times. Sprinkle the chicken with the remaining 1 tablespoon lemon juice after turning for the last time. Cook until chicken is crispy and cooked through, about 30 minutes. Transfer chicken to a platter and keep warm. (The breast pieces will cook faster than the leg and thigh pieces, so watch and remove the breasts when they are cooked through.)

5. Pour the juices accumulated on the platter back into the skillet. Add water. Boil over medium heat. Scrape up the browned bits with a wooden spoon. Let it bubble and thicken. Spoon over chicken.

Makes: 6 servings
Nutrition Facts per serving: 189 cal., 12 g total fat (2 g sat. fat),
63 mg chol., 220 mg sodium, 1 g carbo., 0 g fiber, 19 g pro.
Daily Values: 7% vit. C, 1% calcium, 5% iron

Fricasseed Chicken

A little bit of Italian comfort food, this is a simple and subtle chicken stew. Kids love it served over mashed potatoes with lots of sauce.

1 ½ **pounds skinless, boneless chicken breast halves**

All-purpose flour

2 **tablespoons olive oil**

1 **tablespoon butter**

3 **fresh sage leaves**

3 **tablespoons finely chopped onion**

Salt

Black pepper

⅓ **cup dry red wine or chicken broth**

½ **cup chopped fresh mushrooms**

1. Wash chicken. Pat dry with paper towels. Pour flour into a shallow dish. Coat chicken with flour.

2. Heat a skillet large enough to hold all the chicken breasts in a single layer over medium-high heat until hot. Add oil, butter, and sage and let it get hot. Add chicken to skillet. When well browned on one side, turn chicken over and add the onion. Sprinkle with salt and pepper.

3. When chicken is browned all over and onion is golden, add red wine or chicken broth and mushrooms. Let bubble briskly for a few seconds, then cover skillet and reduce heat to medium-low.

4. Cook chicken at a slow simmer, replenishing cooking juices when they begin to dry out with 2 or 3 tablespoons water. Turn chicken several times and simmer until chicken is tender and cooked through, about 15 minutes. Juices should have condensed into a sauce. If there's not enough sauce, add chicken broth.

Makes: 4 to 6 servings

Nutrition Facts per serving: 321 cal., 12 g total fat (3 g sat. fat), 107 mg chol., 413 mg sodium, 7 g carbo., 1 g fiber, 40 g pro.

Daily Values: 4% vit. A, 4% vit. C, 4% calcium, 9% iron

Chicken with Garlic and Black Pepper

Garlicky, tangy, salty, spicy, and definitely exotic, high-spirited flavors rule in this Thai-influenced chicken dish. The good news is that many of the ingredients are already in your pantry.

4 boneless chicken thighs

1½ teaspoons coarsely ground black pepper

½ cup chopped fresh cilantro

4½ teaspoons soy sauce

1 teaspoon sugar

¼ teaspoon chili powder

4 cloves garlic, minced

2 tablespoons vegetable oil

Brown rice (optional)

Chopped fresh mint, cilantro, and basil

4 lime wedges

1. Wash chicken. Pat dry with paper towels. Rub chicken thighs on both sides with pepper.

2. In a bowl combine the cilantro, soy sauce, sugar, chili powder, and garlic. Rub garlic mixture over the chicken thighs. Marinate in refrigerator for at least 1 hour.

3. Heat oil in a nonstick skillet over medium-high heat until hot. Add chicken pieces, skin side down. Cook until the skin is brown and crisp, about 5 minutes. Turn chicken over. Reduce heat to medium-low and cook for 4 or 5 minutes more or until chicken thighs are cooked through.

4. Transfer chicken to a cutting board, skin side up. Cut each thigh into 3 strips. Serve chicken strips over brown rice if you like, sprinkle with herbs and serve with lime wedges. If desired, you can make a nice sauce by pouring off the excess fat from the skillet and adding ¼ cup water. Boil over medium heat. Scrape up the browned bits with a wooden spoon. Let it bubble and thicken. Spoon over chicken.

Makes: 4 servings

Nutrition Facts per serving: 260 cal., 20 g total fat (5 g sat. fat), 75 mg chol., 407 mg sodium, 3 g carbo., 1 g fiber, 17 g pro. Daily Values: 15% vit. A, 10% vit. C, 2% calcium, 7% iron

Sous Chef Melissa Rodriquez with Chef Chris Canty. They are among the first to attest that it may take ten to fifteen times of offering a menu item to a child before he or she finally tastes it.

oasted Chicken with Orange-Balsamic Glaze

I love balsamic vinegar. It's amazing how much complexity just one ingredient can offer. Mixed with orange juice, it's transformed into the best sauce I know. Kids love the syrupy sauce and smoky taste.

Nonstick cooking spray

1   2½- to 3-pound chicken, cut into 10 pieces

2   tablespoons olive oil

Kosher salt

Freshly ground black pepper

½   cup fresh orange juice

¼   cup balsamic vinegar

1   tablespoon chopped fresh tarragon

1. Preheat oven to 350°F. Spray a baking sheet with cooking spray. Wash chicken. Pat dry with paper towels.

2. Arrange chicken pieces, skin sides up, on the prepared baking sheet. Brush chicken with olive oil. Generously season with salt and pepper. Roast for 30 minutes.

3. Meanwhile, for glaze, in a small saucepan combine the orange juice, balsamic vinegar, and tarragon. Bring to a boil. Reduce heat and simmer, until the liquid is a syrupy consistency.

4. Brush chicken with glaze. Roast until chicken pieces are cooked through, about 15 minutes more.

Makes: 6 servings

Nutrition Facts per serving: 242 cal., 15 g total fat (3 g sat. fat),
66 mg chol., 144 mg sodium, 5 g carbo., 0 g fiber, 21 g pro.
Daily Values: 1% vit. A, 17% vit. C, 2% calcium, 6% iron

Chicken Tikka

Chicken has never been less boring or more sensationally seasoned. This lovely multispiced dish has an Asian pedigree. If it's available in your area, serve it as we often do with TexMati rice, an American version of basmati that's both high quality and a good value.

4   6- to 8-ounce skinless, boneless chicken breast halves

2   cloves garlic, halved

1   2-inch piece fresh ginger, peeled and coarsely chopped

1   cup plain low-fat yogurt

3   tablespoons canola oil

1   lime, juiced (about 4 teaspoons)

1   teaspoon ground cumin

1   teaspoon ground coriander

½   teaspoon ground turmeric

    Salt and black pepper

2   tablespoons canola oil

1   teaspoon butter

1   recipe Simple Steamed Rice (page 168)

    Fresh cilantro (optional)

    Lime wedges (optional)

1. Wash chicken. Pat dry with paper towels. Cut chicken into 1-inch chunks. For marinade, in a blender container combine the garlic and ginger. Blend until finely chopped. Add the yogurt, the 3 tablespoons oil, lime juice, cumin, coriander, and turmeric. Blend until smooth.

2. Pour the marinade over the chicken chunks. Marinate in the refrigerator at least 4 hours. Remove from refrigerator and let stand at room temperature about 30 minutes.

3. Drain chicken, reserving marinade. Season chicken with salt and pepper. Heat the 2 tablespoons oil and the butter in a skillet until hot. Cook and stir the chicken chunks until golden brown and cooked through, 3 to 4 minutes.

4. Meanwhile, bring the reserved marinade to a boil. Serve chicken on top of rice with reserved marinade. If you like, garnish with cilantro and lime wedges.

Makes: 4 servings
Nutrition Facts per serving: 401 cal., 22 g total fat (3 g sat. fat), 105 mg chol., 294 mg sodium, 6 g carbo., 1 g fiber, 43 g pro.
Daily Values: 5% vit. A, 10% vit. C, 15% calcium, 7% iron

Chicken Breasts with Dijon Crust

This was an instant hit because the kids thought the chicken was fried! You won't believe how juicy, tender, and flavorful baked chicken can be until you try this recipe. Proof that it's a winner? When we prepared cod the same way, the kids still thought it was fried chicken and couldn't get enough.

Nonstick cooking spray

6 4-ounce skinless, boneless chicken breast halves

2 tablespoons Dijon mustard

2 tablespoons light sour cream

1 cup fresh bread crumbs

2 teaspoons chopped fresh thyme

1 teaspoon safflower or canola oil

Fine sea salt

Freshly ground black pepper

1. Preheat oven to 425°F. Spray a baking sheet with cooking spray. Wash chicken. Pat dry with paper towels.

2. In a small bowl combine the Dijon mustard and the sour cream. In a shallow dish combine the bread crumbs, thyme, and oil.

3. Season each chicken piece with salt and pepper. Brush the top of each chicken piece with some of the mustard mixture. Dip each chicken piece, mustard side down, into bread crumb mixture, pressing firmly onto chicken.

4. Arrange chicken pieces, coated sides up, on the prepared baking sheet. Bake until the bread crumb mixture is brown and crisp and the chicken is cooked through, about 15 minutes.

Makes: 6 servings
Nutrition Facts per serving: 168 cal., 3 g total fat (1 g sat. fat),
67 mg chol., 287 mg sodium, 4 g carbo., 0 g fiber, 27 g pro.
Daily Values: 1% vit. A, 3% vit. C, 3% calcium, 6% iron

When I first came to Calhoun, the kids were everything from skeptical to reluctant to resistant. Now they are, for the most part, much more open to trying a new taste, to putting something on their plate, to trusting the food and to trusting me. They are so honest and direct about how they feel. I'm just as honest with them about what I believe is good for them.

Chicken Cacciatora

Think of this as Italian comfort food. A sublime dish that looks as beautiful as it tastes, it's even better heated up the day after you cook it. Two hints: Cut peppers in chunks, not slices; and cut the chicken into manageable pieces.

1 3½-pound chicken, cut into 10 pieces

1 tablespoon salt

¼ cup extra-virgin olive oil or canola oil

1 sprig fresh rosemary, needles stripped from stem and chopped

1 clove garlic, minced

1 red bell pepper, cut into 1-inch pieces

1 yellow or green bell pepper, cut into 1-inch pieces

1 medium onion, cut into 1-inch pieces

1 cup canned tomatoes, undrained

1. Wash chicken. Pat dry with paper towels. In a bowl mix salt, 1 tablespoon of the oil, rosemary, and garlic into a paste. Rub paste all over the chicken pieces. Marinate in refrigerator for 1 to 24 hours. Wipe off and reserve the paste from the chicken pieces. Set paste aside.

2. Heat the remaining 3 tablespoons oil in a large skillet until hot. Add chicken to hot oil. Slowly brown the chicken pieces until golden on all sides, about 25 minutes. Make sure pieces don't stick. Transfer chicken to a platter to cool.

3. Pour off any excess fat in skillet and return skillet to heat. Add the bell pepper pieces and onion. Cook and stir until onions begin to brown. Be careful not to burn the delicious glaze that will form on the bottom of the skillet.

4. Return the chicken pieces to the skillet. Stir together the reserved paste and the undrained tomatoes. Pour over chicken in skillet. Simmer, covered, for 10 minutes. Uncover and simmer another 10 minutes. If sauce starts to get a little dry, add about ½ cup water. Chicken should be cooked through and falling off the bone.

Makes: 6 servings

Nutrition Facts per serving: 123 cal., 10 g total fat (1 g sat. fat), 6 mg chol., 1,229 mg sodium, 6 g carbo., 1 g fiber, 3 g pro.
Daily Values: 28% vit. A, 145% vit. C, 2% calcium, 4% iron

Chicken Fajitas

Who doesn't love fajitas? Try this streamlined good-for-you version with all the flavor of TexMex and all the fun of finger food that kids can roll up and eat with their hands. A little messy? Who cares?

8 8-inch flour tortillas

1 pound skinless, boneless chicken thighs

2 teaspoons safflower or canola oil

1 teaspoon fine sea salt

½ teaspoon chili powder

½ teaspoon black pepper

1 tablespoon olive oil

½ onion, thinly sliced

½ red bell pepper, thinly sliced

1 clove garlic, minced

½ teaspoon fresh lime juice

1 recipe Chef Bobo's Simple and Delicious Guacamole (page 48), optional

1. Preheat oven to 250°F. Wrap tortillas tightly in foil that has been sprinkled with water. Place in oven to heat and keep warm.

2. Wash the chicken thighs. Pat dry with paper towels. Cut thighs lengthwise into thin strips.

3. In a bowl combine the safflower or canola oil, salt, chili powder, and black pepper. Add chicken strips, stirring until well coated. Set chicken aside.

4. Heat the olive oil in a skillet until hot. Add the onion, bell pepper, and garlic. Cook and stir until tender. Transfer onion mixture to an ovenproof plate and keep warm in oven.

5. Heat the same skillet over high heat until hot. Add chicken strips to skillet. Cook and stir until golden brown and fully cooked. Remove skillet from heat. Sprinkle lime juice over chicken.

6. Remove the tortillas and the onion mixture from the oven. Place a few of the chicken strips, along with some of the onion mixture, in each tortilla. Roll up. If desired, serve with Chef Bobo's Simple and Delicious Guacamole.

Makes: 4 servings
Nutrition Facts per serving: 382 cal., 15 g total fat (3 g sat. fat),
90 mg chol., 722 mg sodium, 33 g carbo., 2 g fiber, 27 g pro.
Daily Values: 22% vit. A, 52% vit. C, 9% calcium, 19% iron

Chicken and Turkey Kielbasa Jambalaya

A classic New Orleans dish made healthy. The kids at school have always asked for jambalaya because they know I'm from New Orleans. This kid-tailored version uses reduced-fat turkey kielbasa, and it's nowhere near as hot as the original. A bonus: It's great for the cook—a one-pot meal and leftovers (if you have any) are out of this world.

1	2½- to 3-pound chicken, cut into 10 pieces
1	cup chopped onion
1	cup chopped celery
1	cup chopped green bell pepper
2	tablespoons safflower or canola oil
½	pound smoked turkey kielbasa, cut into chunks
1	recipe Seasoning Mix
1	tablespoon minced garlic
½	cup canned tomato sauce
1	cup chopped peeled tomatoes
2 ½	cups Basic Vegetable Stock (page 56)
1 ½	cups uncooked long grain rice

1. Preheat oven to 350°F. Wash chicken. Pat dry with paper towels.

2. In a bowl combine the onion, celery, and bell pepper. Set vegetable mixture aside.

3. Heat oil in an ovenproof pot large enough to hold the rice and chicken until hot. Add the turkey kielbasa and cook until it begins to brown. Remove kielbasa from pot and set aside. Add the chicken pieces to pot, a few at a time, and brown on all sides.

4. Return kielbasa and all of the chicken pieces to pot. Stir in the Seasoning Mix, half of the vegetable mixture, and the garlic. Cook until the vegetables are tender but not brown. Stir in the tomato sauce. Bring to a simmer. Stir in the remaining vegetable mixture along with the chopped tomatoes. Remove pot from heat. Stir in the Basic Vegetable Stock and the uncooked rice.

5. Bake, uncovered, until chicken is cooked through and rice is tender, about 45 minutes. Remove from oven and stir.

Seasoning Mix:
In a small bowl combine 1 tablespoon chopped fresh thyme, 1 tablespoon chopped fresh sage, 1 tablespoon dry mustard, 1½ teaspoons salt, 1 teaspoon paprika, ½ teaspoon black pepper, and 2 bay leaves.

Makes: 6 servings
Nutrition Facts per serving: 492 cal., 19 g total fat (4 g sat. fat),
89 mg chol., 1,036 mg sodium, 47 g carbo., 3 g fiber, 32 g pro.
Daily Values: 19% vit. A, 49% vit. C, 6% calcium, 24% iron

The origin and inspiration for many main dishes may be global and flavors may be complex, but these recipes couldn't be more user-friendly.

Red Beans and Rice with Turkey Kielbasa

What do you cook when both vegetarians and nonvegetarians are seated at your table? Through Step 2, this savory casserole is vegetarian. Adding turkey kielbasa (much healthier than beef kielbasa) makes it a more beloved, authentic New Orleans staple. Prepare it a day ahead and reheat to marry the flavors.

1 pound dry red kidney beans

3 tablespoons olive oil

2 medium onions, finely chopped

1 stalk celery, finely chopped

1 green bell pepper, finely chopped

5 sprigs fresh thyme or 1 teaspoon dried thyme, crushed

2 sprigs fresh oregano or 1 teaspoon dried oregano, crushed

3 bay leaves

1 teaspoon black pepper

2 cloves garlic, minced

3 cups Basic Vegetable Stock (page 56)

1 tablespoon tomato paste

½ teaspoon hot pepper sauce

1 pound smoked turkey kielbasa, cut into chunks

1 recipe Simple Steamed Rice (page 168)

Hot pepper sauce (optional)

1. Rinse beans. In a large soup pot combine beans and 8 cups cold water. Put the beans aside and let sit overnight. (This will make the beans less gaseous and cook faster when ready to cook.) Or you may combine the beans and 8 cups cold water. Bring to a boil. Reduce heat and simmer 2 minutes. Remove soup pot from heat. Let stand for 1 hour. Drain and rinse.

2. Drizzle 2 tablespoons of the oil in a 3-quart soup pot and swirl it around until the oil coats the entire surface. Heat over high heat until hot. Add the onions, celery, bell pepper, thyme, oregano, bay leaves, black pepper, and garlic. Stir around so that the vegetables cook evenly and the flavors mingle. When the vegetables begin to turn brown, stir in the drained beans, the Basic Vegetable Stock, tomato paste, and hot pepper sauce. Bring to a boil. Reduce heat to simmering and cook, covered, for 1 ½ hours, stirring occasionally to make sure there are no beans sticking to the bottom.

3. Meanwhile, drizzle the remaining 1 tablespoon oil in a nonstick skillet and swirl it around until the oil coats the entire surface. Add the turkey kielbasa. Cook and stir until golden brown. Add the kielbasa to the beans. Simmer for 15 minutes more.

4. Check the beans to see if they are fully cooked. They should be firm with no hard core. If so, the beans are done. Season to taste with salt. (You should never season beans with salt before or during cooking because doing so will make the beans tough.) If desired, season with a little more pepper. Remove and discard thyme and oregano sprigs and bay leaves.

5. To serve, put a portion of the Basic Steamed Rice in the middle of a plate or soup bowl. Ladle the bean mixture around it. If desired, sprinkle with additional hot pepper sauce to give it zest.

Makes: 6 to 8 servings

Nutrition Facts per serving with Steamed Rice: 639 cal., 16 g total fat (3 g sat. fat), 47 mg chol., 1,516 mg sodium, 90 g carbo., 21 g fiber, 36 g pro. Daily Values: 6% vit. A, 36% vit. C, 16% calcium, 51% iron

# Asian-Style Turkey Burgers

I've borrowed the flavors from a variety of different Asian cuisines to come up with this recipe. Turkey burgers can be boring. These vibrantly spiced and sweetly sauced burgers are anything but! When they're firm to the touch, they're done. Serve them on a bun or on a bed of rice.

1½ pounds uncooked ground turkey

½ cup chopped scallions

¼ cup soft bread crumbs

3 tablespoons chopped fresh cilantro

2 tablespoons soy sauce

1 tablespoon grated fresh ginger

2 teaspoons finely chopped garlic

Salt

Black pepper

1 teaspoon vegetable oil

½ cup fresh orange juice

2 tablespoons fresh lemon juice

1 tablespoon butter or soy margarine

1. In a bowl combine ground turkey, scallions, bread crumbs, 2 tablespoons of the cilantro, 1 tablespoon of the soy sauce, ginger, and garlic. Season to taste with salt and pepper. Mix well.

2. Divide turkey mixture into 8 equal portions. Shape each portion into a patty about 1 inch thick.

3. Heat oil in a skillet over medium heat until hot. Add 4 of the patties and cook for 7 to 8 minutes. Turn patties over and cook another 8 minutes or until done (165°F). Repeat with remaining 4 patties. Keep the first batch warm in a warm oven.

4. For the sauce, in a small saucepan combine orange juice, lemon juice, and the remaining 1 tablespoon soy sauce. Let bubble until reduced by half. Whisk in the butter and the remaining 1 tablespoon cilantro. Pour over burgers.

Makes: 8 servings

Nutrition Facts per serving: 128 cal., 3 g total fat (1 g sat. fat), 38 mg chol., 388 mg sodium, 4 g carbo., 0 g fiber, 21 g pro.
Daily Values: 4% vit. A, 20% vit. C, 1% calcium, 7% iron

Spaghetti and Turkey Meatballs

Kids love turkey "everything." Happily, it has all the flavor of beef and pork (with less fat), so they never feel deprived. Because the sauce takes a couple of hours, make it the day before. The good news? It isn't high-maintenance because it just simmers. And while it does, your house will be redolent with fragrance and warmth.

3 tablespoons olive oil

½ cup finely chopped onion

1 teaspoon finely chopped garlic

1 pound uncooked ground turkey

1 tablespoon finely chopped fresh oregano

1 teaspoon finely chopped fresh basil

½ cup soft bread crumbs

¼ cup milk

1 egg, beaten

Salt

Black pepper

1 recipe Marinara Sauce

12 ounces dried spaghetti

Olive oil

Grated Parmesan cheese (optional)

1. Heat 1 tablespoon of the oil in a skillet over high heat until hot. Reduce heat to medium. Add onion and garlic. Cook and stir until tender but not brown. Set aside to cool.

2. In a bowl combine the ground turkey, oregano, and basil. Soak the bread crumbs in the milk, then add them to the turkey mixture. Combine the egg and the cooled onion mixture. Add to turkey mixture. Season to taste with salt and pepper. Mix well. Roll the turkey mixture into 1-inch balls. Cover and refrigerate meatballs for 30 minutes.

3. Add the remaining 2 tablespoons oil to skillet and reheat skillet over high heat until hot. Arrange as many meatballs as you can in a single layer in the skillet. Cook until meatballs are browned on all sides, about 15 minutes. Add the cooked meatballs to the Marinara Sauce. Cook for 30 minutes.

4. Meanwhile, cook pasta according to package directions. Drain and toss with a little olive oil. Arrange the cooked pasta in a big bowl or on a serving platter. Pour the Marinara Sauce and meatballs over the pasta and toss. If desired, top each serving with Parmesan cheese.

Marinara Sauce: Pour 2 undrained 28-ounce cans organic tomatoes into a bowl. Crush the tomatoes into small pieces with your hands. Drizzle 1 tablespoon olive oil in a 2-quart saucepan and swirl it around until the oil coats the entire surface. Heat over high heat until hot. Add 1 small onion, finely chopped; 1 stalk celery, finely chopped; ½ small carrot, grated; 1 tablespoon finely chopped garlic; and 1 bay leaf. Cook and stir until tender but not brown. Add tomatoes and juice. Bring to a boil. Reduce heat. Stir in ¼ cup chopped fresh basil, 2 tablespoons chopped fresh oregano, and ⅛ teaspoon red pepper flakes. Simmer for 2 hours.

Makes: 6 servings
Nutrition Facts per serving: 495 cal., 17 g total fat (3 g sat. fat), 83 mg chol., 688 mg sodium, 138 g carbo., 5 g fiber, 21 g pro.
Daily Values: 61% vit. A, 70% vit. C, 16% calcium, 25% iron

Don't be put off by the length of this recipe. It's the perfect family affair! Let your kids get their hands messy rolling meatballs to their hearts' content.

Turkey Meat Loaf

Residing close to the top of the Most Requested List, this good "anytime dish" is one we make often. An unfussy recipe for a mouth-watering meat loaf, it's even better blanketed with a tomato-basil sauce. Leftovers are great reheated or sliced for sandwiches.

Nonstick cooking spray

1 tablespoon olive oil

1 tablespoon butter or soy margarine

1 small onion, finely chopped

1 medium carrot, grated

1 tablespoon chopped garlic

1 tablespoon dry mustard

2 teaspoons salt

2 teaspoons black pepper

1 teaspoon dried thyme, crushed

½ cup uncooked rolled oats or dried bread crumbs

1 large egg, beaten

1½ pounds uncooked ground turkey

1 recipe Tomato-Basil Coulis (page 154)

1. Preheat oven to 350°F. Spray a baking pan or an 8×4×2-inch loaf pan with cooking spray.

2. Heat a nonstick skillet over high heat until hot. Add the olive oil and butter. When the butter has melted, add the onion, carrot, garlic, dry mustard, salt, pepper, and thyme. Cook and stir until tender but not brown. Set aside to cool.

3. In a bowl combine the oats, egg, and the cooled onion mixture. Add ground turkey. Mix well. Shape turkey mixture into a loaf on the prepared baking pan or pat into the prepared loaf pan. Bake until 165°F, about 45 minutes.

4. Let meat loaf stand for 15 minutes. Meanwhile, in a saucepan heat the Tomato-Basil Coulis. Serve meat loaf with coulis ladled over each slice.

Makes: 6 servings
Nutrition Facts per serving: 448 cal., 20 g total fat (4 g sat. fat),
86 mg chol., 1,866 mg sodium, 35 g carbo., 7 g fiber, 35 g pro.
Daily Values: 130% vit. A, 147% vit. C, 21% calcium, 33% iron

Simply Perfect

Making simple dishes is easy. The trick is making simple, healthy, appealing foods that delight your palate and dazzle your taste buds.

Here are some guidelines for cooking food that is so much better for you and your family without sacrificing any flavor or making you feel like a member of the Joyless Nutrition Police.

1. Oven roast, don't fry.
My roasted rutabaga fries (page 178) are irresistible, crunchy, sweet crisp marvels.

2. Prepare more chicken or fish and less red meat.
Choose invigorating flavors, make sure it is beautifully seasoned, and never take the dry, bland, or plain route of preparation.

3. Think natural sugar instead of added sugar.
High-heat roasting brings out the food's natural sweetness. Take advantage of this cooking technique, especially with vegetables.

4. Herbs. The fresher the better. And don't be shy.
Often unsung heroes, a handful of fresh herbs can add amazing power, punch, and depth to even the humblest salad dressing or simplest vegetable. Cook my Roasted Cauliflower (page 201) once and you—and your kids—will be believers.

5. Don't make just vegetables, make vegetable soups.
That's how most kids learn to like vegetables. Who wouldn't like them when they are a harmonious part of a luscious, lovely, warmly simmering soup? Kids also will sing the praises of veggies if they are sauteed in a little olive oil with a few chopped shallots tossed in.

6. Don't think of them as "leftovers."
"Leftovers" sound like something old and cold. But you can easily morph them into a worthy, wonderful, unexpectedly creative and satisfying meal. It's all in the presentation!

7. Diversify. Open your mind. Don't get stuck in a rut.
Experiment, try bold flavors, be bold. You don't need Indian cooking lessons to cook Indian food. Try the Fried Fish Fillets with Indian Flavors (page 155). As your kids experience more diversity on their plates, getting them to try new flavors will become easier.

Individual Pizzas

This isn't just a fail-safe recipe—it's a family activity. Who doesn't love mucking around with their hands, kneading and punching the dough? Not only can you play with your food, you can top it with your favorite cheese or veggie.

I cup water

¾ cup milk

I package dry active yeast

3½ cups all-purpose flour

1½ teaspoons salt

Pizza Toppings*

1. In a saucepan heat water and milk. Cool to lukewarm (105°F to 115°F). Add yeast, whisking until dissolved.

2. Combine flour and salt. Stir yeast mixture into flour mixture. Turn dough out onto a well floured surface. Knead in enough additional flour to form a soft ball. Place the dough in a greased bowl. Cover and let rise at room temperature until doubled in size (about I hour).

3. Preheat oven to 450°F. Punch down the dough and divide it into 6 or 8 equal portions.

4. On a lightly floured surface, roll the dough portions out with a rolling pin, stopping occasionally to stretch the dough slightly with your hands. Continue to roll until you get a nice, even, thin crust. Top dough with whatever toppings you like.

5. Sprinkle cornmeal generously onto 2 large baking sheets. Transfer pizzas to the baking sheets. Bake until dough is golden brown and cheese is melted, 15 to 20 minutes.

*Pizza Toppings:** Top your pizzas with whatever combination of toppings you like. Choose from chopped tomatoes, chopped fresh basil, pizza sauce, grated part-skim mozzarella cheese, minced garlic, thinly sliced onions, cooked ground turkey or ground beef, shredded cooked chicken, and/or thinly sliced vegetables.

Makes: 6 to 8 servings

Nutrition Facts per serving: 327 cal., 5 g total fat (3 g sat. fat), 28 mg chol., 896 mg sodium, 51 g carbo., 3 g fiber, 18 g pro.
Daily Values: 3% vit. A, 6% vit. C, 18% calcium, 20% iron

Parents think it takes longer to cook with their children. My answer? It does take longer. But isn't it worth it? You're sharing invaluable time with your child and passing family traditions to the next generation.

Fish Sticks

Remember the frozen compressed fish sticks we grew up eating? The machine-cut ones that were exactly the same size? These fish sticks aren't remotely like them! While I rarely fry at school, these fresh flounder strips are seasoned, lightly fried, and turn out golden brown and irresistibly crisp every time.

1 **pound flounder fillets**

1 **cup milk**

2 **cups masa harina corn flour or finely ground cornmeal**

2 **teaspoons fine sea salt**

1 **teaspoon black pepper**

Safflower or canola oil

Lemon slices

1 **recipe Tarragon Tartar Sauce (page 25) (optional)**

1. Cut fillets into strips about 1 inch wide and 2 or 3 inches long.

2. Pour the milk into a bowl. Add the fish strips. In a shallow dish combine the corn flour, salt, and pepper. Taste a pinch of the flour mixture to make sure it tastes just a bit salty.

3. Remove the fish strips from the milk, letting the excess drip off. Toss fish strips in the flour mixture until well coated.

4. Pour oil into a large saucepan. The oil should not come more than halfway up the side of the saucepan. Heat oil to 335°F. Fry fish strips, a few at a time, until crisp and golden brown, about 3 minutes. (Take care not to put too many fish strips in the saucepan. Overcrowding will greatly reduce the temperature of the oil. Also be careful not to splash any of the hot oil on you.) Drain fish on paper towels. Serve with lemon slices, and, if you like, dip in Tarragon Tartar Sauce.

Makes: 4 servings
Nutrition Facts per serving: 276 cal., 14 g total fat (2 g sat. fat),
67 mg chol., 467 mg sodium, 16 g carbo., 3 g fiber, 24 g pro.
Daily Values: 3% vit. A, 35% vit. C, 9% calcium, 6% iron

flounder Fajitas

A great TexMex way to prepare fish—seasoned and sizzling! Because there is no "fishy" taste, your kids—even the toughest critics—will eat them. A note of caution: Although I always prefer fresh fish, it's particularly important for this recipe. Frozen flounder is too waterlogged.

8	8-inch flour tortillas
1	pound flounder fillets
2	teaspoons safflower or canola oil
1	teaspoon ground cumin
1	teaspoon fine sea salt
½	teaspoon chili powder
½	teaspoon black pepper
1	tablespoon olive oil
½	onion, thinly sliced
½	red bell pepper, thinly sliced
1	clove garlic, minced
½	teaspoon fresh lime juice
1	recipe Chef Bobo's Simple and Delicious Guacamole (page 48) (optional)

1. Preheat oven to 250°F. Wrap tortillas tightly in foil that has been sprinkled with water. Place in oven to heat and keep warm.

2. Cut fillets into strips about 1 inch wide and 2 or 3 inches long. Combine the safflower oil, cumin, salt, chili powder, and black pepper. Rub oil mixture over fish strips until well coated. Set fish aside.

3. Heat the olive oil in a nonstick skillet until hot. Add the onion, bell pepper, and garlic. Cook and stir until tender. Transfer onion mixture to an ovenproof plate and keep warm in oven.

4. Heat the same skillet over medium heat until hot. Add the fish strips to skillet. Cook and stir fish until firm and opaque. Remove skillet from the heat. Sprinkle lime juice over fish.

5. Remove the tortillas and the onion mixture from the oven. Place a few of the fish strips, along with some of the onion mixture, in each tortilla. Roll up. If you like, serve with Chef Bobo's Simple and Delicious Guacamole.

Makes: 4 servings

Nutrition Facts per serving: 333 cal., 11 g total fat (2 g sat. fat), 48 mg chol., 706 mg sodium, 32 g carbo., 2 g fiber, 24 g pro.
Daily Values: 20% vit. A, 44% vit. C, 10% calcium, 14% iron

oasted Salmon with Honey and Soy Glaze

I learned how to prepare this dish at the French Culinary Institute where I fell in love with pan-roasting. A mahogany-color, Asian-inspired rich glaze coats the salmon. Because kids love soy and honey, it's bound to be a hit with everyone at your dinner table.

¼ cup soy sauce

1 teaspoon grated fresh ginger

¼ cup honey

2 tablespoons extra-virgin olive oil or canola oil

1 pound skinless, boneless salmon fillets

1. Preheat oven to 350°F.

2. For glaze, in a small saucepan combine the soy sauce and ginger. Bring to a simmer. Stir in the honey until combined. Remove saucepan from heat.

3. Drizzle oil in an ovenproof nonstick skillet large enough to hold all the salmon, and swirl it around until the oil coats the entire surface. Heat over high heat until hot.

4. Reduce heat to medium. Add the salmon fillets to the hot skillet. Cook until the fish turns pink and opaque halfway up from the bottom. (The bottom of the fillets should be browning.) Remove skillet from heat. Turn fillets over and brush with glaze. Transfer skillet to oven. Bake until firm, about 5 minutes.

Makes: 4 servings
Nutrition Facts per serving: 265 cal., 11 g total fat (2 g sat. fat), 59 mg chol., 1,097 mg sodium, 17 g carbo., 0 g fiber, 25 g pro.
Daily Values: 2% vit. A, 2% calcium, 6% iron

Fish was one of our first tough-sell items at Calhoun. We tried every tactic known to sell it, including singing the praises of fish, promising seconds on a favorite side dish, and shamelessly pointing out how much their peers were enjoying it.

Baked Codfish with Soy-Mustard Sauce

Chef Tomek came up with this unusual Asian-flavored dish, and it was love at first bite. All kids love soy sauce because they are so familiar with Chinese food, so we don't hear much "Yuck, fish!" when this is on the menu.

Nonstick cooking spray

4 4-ounce codfish fillets

1 tablespoon vegetable or olive oil

Fine sea salt

Black pepper

1 recipe Soy-Mustard Sauce

1. Preheat oven to 350°F. Spray a baking sheet with cooking spray.

2. Brush the fillets lightly with oil. Season to taste with salt and pepper. Arrange fish on prepared baking sheet. Bake until just beginning to brown, 7 to 8 minutes. Brush tops with some of the Soy-Mustard Sauce. Bake until firm and opaque, 2 to 3 minutes more.

Soy-Mustard Sauce:
In a bowl combine 2 tablespoons Dijon mustard, 1 tablespoon soy sauce, 1 tablespoon grated fresh ginger, 1 tablespoon finely chopped shallot, and 1 teaspoon sherry vinegar. Whisk in ¼ cup canola oil.

Makes: 4 servings
Nutrition Facts per serving: 169 cal., 9 g total fat (1 g sat. fat), 49 mg chol., 351 mg sodium, 0 g carbo., 0 g fiber, 21 g pro.
Daily Values: 1% vit. A, 2% vit. C, 2% calcium, 2% iron

Dijon-Crusted Striped Bass

This recipe uses the same technique as Chicken Breasts with Dijon Crust (page 132). It works well on any sturdy fish (bass and cod, for example) and comes out so juicy and toothsome that there's nothing remotely "fishy" about it. Serve it with a squeeze of lemon and tartar sauce.

Nonstick cooking spray

1 tablespoon Dijon mustard

1 tablespoon light sour cream

1 cup dry bread crumbs

2 teaspoons chopped fresh thyme

4 4-ounce striped bass fillets

Fine sea salt

Black pepper

Lemon slices

1. Preheat oven to 400°F. Spray a baking sheet with cooking spray.

2. In a bowl combine the mustard and sour cream. In a shallow dish combine the bread crumbs and thyme.

3. Brush the top of each fillet with the mustard mixture. Press each fillet, mustard side down, into the bread crumb mixture, pressing firmly onto fish. Season to taste with salt and pepper.

4. Arrange fish on the prepared baking sheet, coated side up. Bake until firm, opaque, and coating begins to turn golden brown, about 7 to 8 minutes. Serve with lemon slices.

Makes: 4 servings

Nutrition Facts per serving: 153 cal., 3 g total fat (1 g sat. fat), 92 mg chol., 328 mg sodium, 7 g carbo., 0 g fiber, 21 g pro.
Daily Values: 3% vit. A, 13% vit. C, 4% calcium, 8% iron

C ajun Catfish

One of our chefs at Calhoun, Ilya Malachias, introduced this fish entrée when I asked the chefs to explore "oven frying" fish and chicken instead of deep frying. This flavorful and crispy catfish dish was such a hit! Serve it with the Tarragon Tartar Sauce (page 25) and a little squeeze of fresh lemon.

Nonstick cooking spray

1 cup buttermilk

1 teaspoon hot pepper sauce

1 pound catfish fillets

1 cup dry bread crumbs

1 tablespoon dried thyme, crushed

1 tablespoon dry mustard

1 tablespoon salt

1 teaspoon garlic powder

1 teaspoon onion powder

1 teaspoon paprika

1 teaspoon black pepper

¼ cup safflower or canola oil

1. Preheat oven to 425°F. Spray a baking sheet with cooking spray.

2. In a bowl combine the buttermilk and hot pepper sauce. Place the fillets in the buttermilk mixture.

3. In a shallow dish combine the bread crumbs, thyme, mustard, salt, garlic powder, onion powder, paprika, and pepper. Stir in the oil.

4. Remove fish fillets from buttermilk mixture, letting the excess drip off. Dip the fish in the bread crumb mixture, pressing firmly onto fish. Arrange fish on the prepared baking sheet.

5. Bake until firm, opaque, and coating begins to turn golden brown, about 10 minutes.

Makes: 4 servings
Nutrition Facts per serving: 336 cal., 23 g total fat (3 g sat. fat), 54 mg chol., 1,216 mg sodium, 12 g carbo., 2 g fiber, 20 g pro.
Daily Values: 8% vit. A, 37% vit. C, 8% calcium, 10% iron

The crunch, the bold flavors, and the texture—they all work together to make this dish much more than just another fish recipe.

Roasted Codfish with Tomato-Basil Coulis

Coulis is simply pureed tomatoes, cooked down. It just sounds better in French! Cod is a strong fish and its flavor can stand up to a robust tomato sauce. If you're considering trying out fish on your family, this is the recipe to make. I think kids love cod because it looks enough like a chicken breast to be reassuringly familiar!

Nonstick cooking spray

1 pound codfish fillets

1 tablespoon extra-virgin olive oil or canola oil

Fine sea salt

Black pepper

1 recipe Tomato-Basil Coulis

1. Preheat oven to 350°F. Spray a baking sheet with cooking spray.

2. Brush fillets lightly with oil. Season to taste with salt and pepper. Arrange fish on prepared baking sheet.

3. Bake for 3 minutes. Turn fillets over and bake until firm, opaque, and just beginning to brown, about 5 minutes more. Serve with Tomato-Basil Coulis.

Tomato-Basil Coulis:

In a saucepan combine ⅓ cup dry red wine and 2 teaspoons balsamic vinegar. Simmer until reduced by half. Cool. In a blender container combine one 28-ounce can organic tomatoes, drained; 1 cup fresh basil leaves; and ⅓ cup extra-virgin olive oil or canola oil. Blend until pureed. Add the reduced wine mixture. Blend until combined. Season to taste with salt and black pepper. Store leftover sauce in a tightly covered container in the refrigerator.

Makes: 4 servings

Nutrition Facts per serving: 387 cal., 24 g total fat (3 g sat. fat), 48 mg chol., 893 mg sodium, 20 g carbo., 5 g fiber, 24 g pro.
Daily Values: 58% vit. A, 108% vit. C, 16% calcium, 18% iron

 ried Fish Fillets with Indian Flavors

At once sweet, smoky, tart, tangy, and light, these fillets are easy to make and not the least bit greasy. A delicious way to teach kids about Indian cuisine.

1 teaspoon ground turmeric

½ teaspoon salt

1 pound tilapia or flounder fillets

1 tablespoon fresh lime or lemon juice

1 teaspoon minced garlic

1 teaspoon chopped fresh ginger

1 teaspoon ground coriander

1 teaspoon ground cumin

¼ teaspoon ground ginger

Salt

Black pepper

1 cup all-purpose flour

1 cup semolina flour

2 egg whites

½ cup plus 1 tablespoon canola or safflower oil

1 recipe Chile Sauce (optional)

Lime or lemon wedges

1. Combine turmeric and the ½ teaspoon salt. Rub over the fish fillets until well coated on both sides.

2. With a mortar and pestle, make a paste of the lime or lemon juice, garlic, fresh ginger, coriander, cumin, and ground ginger. Rub all sides of the fish fillets with the paste. Season to taste with salt and pepper. Place fish on a plate and refrigerate at least 30 minutes.

3. When ready to cook, place the all-purpose flour in a shallow dish and the semolina flour in another shallow dish.

4. Beat the egg whites with the 1 tablespoon canola oil. Coat each fish fillet with the all-purpose flour, dip in the beaten egg white mixture, then coat again with the semolina flour.

5. Pour the ½ cup canola oil into a skillet large enough to hold all the fillets in a single layer. Heat over high heat until hot. Reduce heat to medium. Add fish to hot oil. Fry fillets until golden brown, about 2 minutes. Turn each fillet over and fry on the other side until crisp and golden brown. Drain on paper towels. Serve with Chile Sauce, if you like, and lime or lemon wedges.

Chile Sauce:
Combine ½ cup organic ketchup, 4 ½ teaspoons lime or lemon juice, 1 tablespoon chopped fresh cilantro, and 1 teaspoon chopped fresh jalapeño chile pepper. If your family likes it spicier, add a few drops hot pepper sauce.

Makes: 4 servings
Nutrition Facts per serving: 502 cal., 18 g total fat (1 g sat. fat),
0 mg chol., 521 mg sodium, 56 g carbo., 3 g fiber, 29 g pro.
Daily Values: 1% vit. A, 6% vit. C, 6% calcium, 27% iron

Scallops with Lemon, Garlic, and Capers

This is the recipe I'm most likely to make at home if I have guests. My friends love it because it's a medley of flavors: fresh, tart, salty, and garlicky. The recipe tester thought it delightful: "I almost cried, it was so good!"

1 ½ pounds sea scallops

Salt

Black pepper

2 tablespoons butter or soy margarine

1 tablespoon minced garlic

¼ cup extra-virgin olive oil or canola oil

2 tablespoons capers, drained

¼ cup fresh lemon juice

2 tablespoons chopped fresh parsley

1. Season the scallops with salt and pepper. Set aside. Heat a nonstick skillet big enough to hold all the scallops in a single layer over high heat until hot. Add butter. Place scallops in skillet, 1 at a time, on one of their flat sides. Let brown, then add the garlic. Let garlic begin to caramelize, then add the oil and capers.

2. Turn each scallop over, browned side up. Add the lemon juice and 1 tablespoon of the parsley. Cook, covered, until scallops turn opaque, about 5 minutes more.

3. Spoon lemon-garlic mixture over scallops. Sprinkle with the remaining 1 tablespoon parsley.

Makes: 4 servings
Nutrition Facts per serving: 335 cal., 21 g total fat (6 g sat. fat),
73 mg chol., 611 mg sodium, 7 g carbo., 0 g fiber, 29 g pro.
Daily Values: 8% vit. A, 25% vit. C, 6% calcium, 5% iron

Some of the students from the high school cooking class enjoy cooking so much, they help in the kitchen during lunch service.

156

# Baked Shrimp with Tomatoes and Parmesan Cheese

A savory international dish, it marries fresh shrimp (you can substitute cod or red snapper) with invigorating Mediterranean flavors for a warmly satisfying family dinner.

1 tablespoon olive oil

1 teaspoon finely chopped shallot

1 clove garlic, minced

1 cup chopped plum tomatoes

2 tablespoons chopped fresh basil

1 teaspoon fine sea salt

Freshly ground black pepper

1 pound shrimp, peeled and deveined

½ cup shredded Parmesan cheese

1 teaspoon chopped fresh parsley

1. Preheat oven to 350°F.

2. Heat oil in an ovenproof skillet large enough to hold all the shrimp over high heat until hot. Reduce heat to medium. Add shallot and garlic. Cook and stir until tender. Add the tomatoes and basil. Cook and stir until the tomatoes are soft and much of the liquid has evaporated. Stir in salt. Season to taste with pepper. Remove skillet from heat. Stir shrimp into skillet, then lay them out flat and neat in the skillet. Sprinkle with Parmesan cheese.

3. Transfer skillet to oven. Bake until shrimp turn pink and opaque, about 10 minutes. Remove from oven. Sprinkle with parsley.

Makes: 4 servings
Nutrition Facts per serving: 439 cal., 24 g total fat (12 g sat. fat),
220 mg chol., 1,703 mg sodium, 6 g carbo., 1 g fiber, 49 g pro.
Daily Values: 19% vit. A, 19% vit. C, 90% calcium, 19% iron

Shrimp Sautéed with Garlic and Black Pepper

I first discovered this recipe in Thailand. Similar to Chicken with Garlic and Black Pepper (page 128)—the same intense herbs, spices, and quick preparation—I never tire of it.

1 pound large shrimp, peeled and deveined

1 ½ teaspoons coarsely ground black pepper

¼ cup chopped fresh cilantro

1 tablespoon soy sauce

1 teaspoon sugar

¼ teaspoon chili powder

2 cloves garlic, minced

2 tablespoons vegetable oil

Lime wedges

1. Rub shrimp on all sides with pepper. Set aside.

2. In a bowl combine the cilantro, soy sauce, sugar, chili powder, and garlic. Pour cilantro mixture over shrimp. Marinate in refrigerator for at least 1 hour.

3. Heat oil in a nonstick skillet over medium-high heat. Add shrimp. Cook and stir until shrimp turn pink and opaque, about 5 minutes. Serve with lime wedges.

Makes: 4 servings

Nutrition Facts per serving: 194 cal., 9 g total fat (1 g sat. fat),
172 mg chol., 403 mg sodium, 4 g carbo., 0 g fiber, 24 g pro.
Daily Values: 13% vit. A, 11% vit. C, 7% calcium, 19% iron

Farfalle with Garden Vegetables and Cheese

A quick, colorful, easy, unbeatable summer dish that is so flexible. If you like, add chopped radicchio, romaine, or arugula or throw in some toasted pine nuts just before you serve it and you'll get raves every time.

12 ounces dried farfalle pasta

2 cups fresh basil leaves

½ cup grated Parmesan cheese

⅓ cup extra-virgin olive oil or canola oil

2 cloves garlic, smashed

1 cup green beans, cut into 2-inch pieces

1 small red onion, halved and thinly sliced

1 cup pear-shaped yellow tomatoes

1 cup pear-shaped red tomatoes

Grated Parmesan cheese

1. Cook pasta according to package directions.

2. Meanwhile, in a blender container combine basil leaves, Parmesan cheese, oil, and garlic. Blend until smooth.

3. In a saucepan bring ½ cup salted water to a boil. Add green beans and cook for 2 minutes. The beans should be fully cooked but still have a little snap to them. Drain beans in a colander and immediately shock them in ice cold water to retain their green color. Remove from cold water and add onion slices to colander.

4. Drain the pasta, pouring the hot water over the green beans and onion slices in colander. Pour pasta into a large bowl. Pour the basil mixture over the pasta. Add the tomatoes, green beans, and onion slices. Toss together. Sprinkle with additional cheese.

Makes: 6 servings
Nutrition Facts per serving: 390 cal., 17 g total fat (4g sat. fat), 10 mg chol., 287 mg sodium, 49 g carbo., 3 g fiber, 13 g pro.
Daily Values: 29% vit. A, 29% vit. C, 19% calcium, 15% iron

Farfalle looks like tiny butterflies or little bow ties—it's the pasta that makes kids smile before they even taste it!

 acaroni and Cheese

Delicious? No, addictive. Next to fried chicken this is the runaway favorite at school (not just with kids but with the faculty too!). The secret is the Dijon mustard, which brings out the cheese taste and keeps it from being bland. You will never need another recipe for macaroni and cheese.

1	pound dried elbow macaroni
3	tablespoons olive oil
3	tablespoons all-purpose flour
3	cups cold milk
2	cups grated cheddar cheese
2	teaspoons Dijon mustard
½	teaspoon hot pepper sauce
	Salt
	Freshly ground black pepper

1. Cook pasta according to package directions. Drain. Preheat oven to 350°F.

2. Heat oil in a 3-quart saucepan over high heat until hot. Reduce heat to medium. Add the flour, stirring constantly until it just starts to turn a light beige. Add the milk a little at a time. With each addition, whisk the flour and milk together until well combined. (You will see that, at first, it will become very thick like a paste, but it will thin as you gradually add the milk.) After you have added all the milk, let the sauce come to a bubbling simmer.

3. Add 1½ cups of the cheese and the mustard. Whisk until it is completely melted into the sauce. If the sauce seems too thick, add more milk until you get a consistency that is smooth and will pour easily. Stir in the hot pepper sauce. Season to taste with salt and pepper.

4. Pour the cooked macaroni into a baking pan large enough to hold all the pasta and sauce. Pour the sauce over the macaroni and stir until combined. Sprinkle the remaining ½ cup cheese over the top. Bake until heated through and lightly browned on top, about 25 minutes.

Note: If you like, add tomatoes, tuna, peas or chunks of ham to the macaroni and cheese before baking.

Makes: 6 servings
Nutrition Facts per serving: 592 cal., 25 g total fat (12 g sat. fat),
56 mg chol., 475 mg sodium, 65 g carbo., 2 g fiber, 25 g pro.
Daily Values: 14% vit. A, 2% vit. C, 48% calcium, 15% iron

# Fusilli with Tomatoes, Basil, and Mozzarella Cheese

This is a great recipe for summer when fresh tomatoes are ripe and delicious. In the winter, when tomatoes may not be as good, use canned tomatoes that have been drained of their liquid and chopped. A sprinkle of red pepper flakes adds a nice zest to this dish.

1	pound dried fusilli pasta
2	tablespoons extra-virgin olive oil or canola oil
2	pounds fresh tomatoes, seeded and chopped
½	cup fresh basil leaves, coarsely chopped
	Salt and black pepper
1	cup shredded fresh mozzarella cheese

1. Cook pasta according to package directions. Drain. Let pasta stand until room temperature. Transfer pasta to a large bowl. Add the olive oil, tossing to coat. Add the tomatoes and basil. Season to taste with salt and pepper. Toss together. Sprinkle with cheese.

Makes: 4 servings
Nutrition Facts per serving: 597 cal., 14 g total fat (4 g sat. fat), 16 mg chol., 299 mg sodium, 96 g carbo., 5 g fiber, 23 g pro.
Daily Values: 33% vit. A, 67% vit. C, 22% calcium, 25% iron

# Mexican Tomato Rice

Rice and beans at its best: cumin-scented, cilantro-spiked, colorful, healthful, quick, vegetarian, and only one pot to wash! Sprinkle with white cheddar or Monterey Jack while it bakes if you want a richer dish.

1	28-ounce can plum tomatoes, undrained
1	bay leaf
	Salt
	Black pepper
2	tablespoons olive oil
1	small onion, finely chopped
2	fresh jalapeño chile peppers, seeded and finely chopped
1	red bell pepper, finely chopped
1	tablespoon minced garlic
1	teaspoon ground turmeric
1	teaspoon ground cumin
1 ½	cups jasmine rice
1 ½	cups canned organic red kidney or black beans, drained and rinsed
2	tablespoon chopped fresh cilantro

1. Preheat oven to 350°F.

2. Place the undrained tomatoes in a blender container. Blend until smooth. Transfer to a saucepan, adding enough water to blended mixture to equal 3 cups. Add bay leaf to saucepan. Season to taste with salt and pepper. Bring to a boil.

3. Heat oil in an ovenproof 2-quart saucepan until hot. Add onion, chile peppers, bell pepper, garlic, turmeric, and cumin. Cook and stir until the liquid has evaporated. Add rice, scraping the bottom with a large spatula to prevent burning. Add the tomato liquid and beans. Bring to a boil. Remove from heat.

4. Transfer saucepan to oven. Bake, covered, until rice is done, about 20 minutes. Remove bay leaf. Stir in cilantro.

Makes: 4 servings

Nutrition Facts per serving: 323 cal., 7 g total fat (1 g sat. fat), 0 mg chol., 446 mg sodium, 55 g carbo., 10 g fiber, 11 g pro.
Daily Values: 59% vit. A, 137% vit. C, 12% calcium, 22% iron

Chef Ilya Malachias, who grew up in a New Orleans food family, says, "Food is like language. If you pick it up early, it's just easier and more natural."

sensationally seasoned veggies bo

Serve a plain steamed vegetable and kids will head for the door without a bite. Vegetables need to be braised, glazed, roasted, sautéed, and caramelized to enhance their natural flavor.

 imple Steamed Rice

This technique results in the best steamed rice! It's unequivocally better than any boxed mix you've ever tried. Sautéing the rice in oil first makes all the difference; it brings out the full nutty flavor of the grain. Once you've tasted this, you'll never cook rice any other way.

1 tablespoon safflower or canola oil

1 ½ cups uncooked long grain white or basmati rice

1 teaspoon kosher salt

2½ cups water or Basic Vegetable Stock (page 56)

1. Drizzle the oil in a 1-quart saucepan and swirl it around until the oil coats the entire surface. Heat over high heat until hot.

2. Add the rice to the hot oil and stir it around until the rice aroma begins to waft up and smells like toasted rice. Stir in the salt.

3. Slowly and carefully add the water (it will spatter because the pan and ingredients are hot). Bring to boiling. Reduce heat to low. Simmer, covered, for 17 minutes.

4. Remove saucepan from heat. Fluff the rice with a fork. Let stand, covered, for 10 minutes before serving.

Makes: 6 servings
Nutrition Facts per serving: 189 cal., 3 g total fat (0 g sat. fat),
0 mg chol., 327 mg sodium, 37 g carbo., 1 g fiber, 3 g pro.
Daily Values: 2% calcium, 11% iron

Coconut Rice

Way beyond basic rice, this flavorful Thai dish goes beautifully with just about any entrée. It's especially good with Chicken with Garlic and Black Pepper (page 128).

1 tablespoon safflower or canola oil

1 ½ cups uncooked long grain white or basmati rice

1 teaspoon kosher salt

1 ½ cups water

1 cup canned unsweetened coconut milk

1. Drizzle the oil in a 1-quart saucepan and swirl it around until the oil coats the entire surface. Heat over high heat until hot.

2. Add the rice to the hot oil and stir it around until the rice aroma begins to waft up and smells like toasted rice. Stir in the salt.

3. Slowly and carefully add the water and coconut milk (it will spatter because the pan and ingredients are hot). Bring to boiling. Reduce heat to low. Simmer, covered, for 17 minutes.

4. Remove saucepan from heat. Fluff the rice with a fork. Let stand, covered, for 10 minutes before serving.

Makes: 6 servings
Nutrition Facts per serving: 262 cal., 9 g total fat (7 g sat. fat),
0 mg chol., 333 mg sodium, 38 g carbo., 1 g fiber, 4 g pro.
Daily Values: 1% calcium, 13% iron

Couscous with Roasted Vegetables

A medley of sweetly roasted vegetables tossed with a bed of airy couscous, this is one of those side dishes so complete and flavorful it could easily stand on its own. North African in origin, it's equally delicious served hot or at room temperature.

Nonstick cooking spray

1 small eggplant, peeled and cut into 1-inch pieces

1 medium zucchini, cut into 1-inch pieces

1 red bell pepper, cut into 1-inch pieces

1 small red onion, cut into 1-inch pieces

2 tablespoons extra-virgin olive oil or canola oil

Kosher salt

Black pepper

2 cups water

1 teaspoon kosher salt

2 ½ cups plain uncooked couscous

1 teaspoon extra-virgin olive oil or canola oil

1. Preheat oven to 400°F. Spray a baking sheet with cooking spray.

2. Put the eggplant, zucchini, bell pepper, and onion in a large bowl. Add the 2 tablespoons olive oil and toss. Make sure all pieces are coated with oil. Sprinkle generously with salt and pepper. Spread the vegetables in a single layer on the prepared baking sheet. Roast about 15 minutes or until golden brown.

3. Meanwhile, in a small saucepan bring water and the 1 teaspoon salt to boiling. Pour the couscous in a bowl and stir in the 1 teaspoon olive oil. Pour the boiling water over the couscous, stirring constantly so it won't clump. Cover with plastic wrap and let stand for 30 minutes.

4. Transfer couscous to a serving platter and top with roasted vegetables.

Makes: 4 to 6 servings
Nutrition Facts per serving: 540 cal., 9 g total fat (1 g sat. fat), 0 mg chol., 562 mg sodium, 98 g carbo., 9 g fiber, 16 g pro.
Daily Values: 38% vit. A, 105% vit. C, 5% calcium, 10% iron

"I know it sounds hokey, but food tastes better when it's made with love. Skill is far less important than love."

Quinoa Pilaf with Crimini Mushrooms

This nutty-flavored pilaf is a big hit at Calhoun. Kids are fascinated to learn that quinoa is not a grain but a Peruvian seed. It looks, acts, and cooks like a grain, but after it's cooked you can tell it's a seed because you can actually see the stamen inside. If you can't find quinoa in your supermarket, check a health store or gourmet market.

1 tablespoon olive oil

1 shallot, finely chopped

½ cup fresh crimini mushrooms, thinly sliced

1½ cups quinoa, rinsed and drained

1½ teaspoons kosher salt

½ teaspoon snipped fresh thyme

1 bay leaf

Freshly ground black pepper

3 cups Basic Vegetable Stock (page 56) or water

1. Drizzle oil in a saucepan and swirl it around until the oil coats the entire surface. Heat over high heat until hot. Reduce heat to medium and add the shallot and mushrooms. Cook and stir until shallot is tender and mushrooms are brown.

2. Stir the quinoa, salt, thyme, bay leaf, and pepper into the saucepan. Let the ingredients heat up and roast a little to bring out their fullest flavors. The steam coming up should be very aromatic.

3. Slowly and carefully add the Basic Vegetable Stock (it will spatter because the pan and ingredients are hot). Bring to boiling. Reduce heat to low. Simmer, covered, for 15 minutes.

4. Remove saucepan from heat. Remove bay leaf. Fluff the quinoa with a fork. Let stand, covered, about 10 minutes before serving.

Makes: 4 servings

Nutrition Facts per serving: 291 cal., 8 g total fat (1 g sat. fat),
0 mg chol., 871 mg sodium, 48 g carbo., 4 g fiber, 10 g pro.
Daily Values: 4% vit. A, 1% vit. C, 4% calcium, 34% iron

rzo with Garlic and Fresh Herbs

Kids love orzo because it's like pasta wearing a rice costume! In this effortless recipe orzo is simply suffused with fresh chopped herbs and garlic. One caution: it cooks faster than rice, so take it off the stove when it's still al dente.

4 cups water

12 ounces dried orzo

1 tablespoon kosher salt

2 tablespoons extra-virgin olive oil or canola oil

1 teaspoon chopped fresh basil

1 teaspoon chopped fresh parsley

1 teaspoon chopped fresh mint

1 clove garlic, minced

Freshly ground black pepper

1. In a saucepan bring water to boiling. Add the orzo and salt. Boil, uncovered, about 8 minutes or until the orzo is al dente (tender but still firm).

2. Meanwhile, in a large bowl mix the olive oil, basil, parsley, mint, and garlic. Drain orzo and toss it together with the herb mixture. Season generously with pepper.

Makes: 4 servings

Nutrition Facts per serving: 377 cal., 8 g total fat (1 g sat. fat), 0 mg chol., 488 mg sodium, 64 g carbo., 2 g fiber, 11 g pro.
Daily Values: 2% vit. C, 2% calcium, 19% iron

Oven Roasted Potatoes with Onions

If you've never tried this technique for cooking potatoes, trust me, after you eat this dish, you'll want to use it every time. With very little input from you, the potatoes turn out crispy and salty, crunchy on the outside, creamy on the inside.

Nonstick cooking spray

1 pound tiny new red potatoes

1 small red onion, thinly sliced

1 sprig fresh rosemary, needles stripped from the stem

2 tablespoons olive oil

Kosher salt

Freshly ground black pepper

1. Preheat oven to 400°F. Spray a baking sheet with cooking spray.

2. Cut potatoes into quarters. Put the potatoes, onion, and rosemary needles in a large bowl. Add the olive oil and toss together. Make sure all pieces are coated with oil. Sprinkle generously with salt and pepper.

3. Place the potatoes and onion in a single layer on the prepared baking sheet. Roast for 15 to 20 minutes. The potatoes are done when they are golden brown and a knife will easily cut through 1 of the wedges.

Makes: 4 servings
Nutrition Facts per serving: 129 cal., 7 g total fat (1 g sat. fat), 0 mg chol., 67 mg sodium, 15 g carbo., 2 g fiber, 2 g pro.
Daily Values: 24% vit. C, 2% calcium, 7% iron

Some of our young vegetarians have been very instrumental in improving our salad bar.

Oven French Fries

These oven-roasted potatoes look, act, and taste like french fries that are actually fried, and they're the only french fry we make at Calhoun. Personally, I think they have more flavor and are crispier. How good are they? The kids at school never complain!

Nonstick cooking spray

2 or 3 baking potatoes

2 tablespoons safflower or canola oil

Salt

Black pepper

1. Preheat oven to 425°F. Spray a baking sheet with cooking spray.

2. Slice the potatoes lengthwise into "french fry shapes" ($\frac{1}{2}$-inch-wide strips). Put the potato strips in a large bowl and drizzle with oil. Toss w ell so that each piece of potato is coated with oil. Sprinkle generously with salt and pepper. Place the potato strips in a single layer on the prepared baking sheet.

3. Bake about 20 minutes or until golden brown. Season to taste with salt and pepper.

Makes: 4 to 6 servings

Nutrition Facts per serving: 123 cal., 7 g total fat (0 g sat. fat),
0 mg chol., 79 mg sodium, 14 g carbo., 1 g fiber, 2 g pro.
Daily Values: 22% vit. C, 1% calcium, 7% iron

Keys to Vegetable Success

Purchase fresh vegetables when they're in season (as much as possible). Kids respond best to the texture of fresh produce, even after cooking.

Season them well while cooking. Use olive oil, not butter. Don't be shy about tossing in some fresh herbs and spices. Add chopped shallot—they're sweeter than onion—and drizzle with a little vinegar.

Don't stick to basics—kids love to be surprised. Try new vegetable combinations and different cooking techniques. Roasting vegetables makes them sweeter. Grilling veggies adds a smoky flavor.

Rutabaga Fries

This is the dish that convinced everyone at Calhoun that "fries" don't have to be made out of potatoes or cooked in vats of oil to be fabulous. In fact, they don't even have to be fried! We oven-fry rutabaga strips in a very hot oven, and, like our french fries, they turn out crisp and delicious.

Nonstick cooking spray

2 pounds rutabagas, peeled

¼ cup canola oil or olive oil

1 tablespoon salt

1 teaspoon black pepper

1. Preheat oven to 425°F. Spray a baking sheet with cooking spray.

2. Slice the rutabagas lengthwise into "french fry shapes" (½-inch-wide strips). Put the rutabaga strips in a large bowl and drizzle with oil. Toss well so that each piece of rutabaga is coated with oil. Sprinkle fries with salt and pepper. Place rutabaga strips in a single layer on the prepared baking sheet.

3. Bake about 20 minutes or until golden brown. (Watch carefully because rutabagas have more sugar in them than baking potatoes and tend to caramelize faster. If the fries are getting too dark too fast, reduce the oven temperature to 400°F.) Season to taste.

Makes: 4 servings
Nutrition Facts per serving: 191 cal., 14 g total fat (1 g sat. fat), 0 mg chol., 1,783 mg sodium, 16 g carbo., 5 g fiber, 2 g pro.
Daily Values: 20% vit. A, 60% vit. C, 9% calcium, 6% iron

Rutabagas are my first choice for these fries although you can make fries out of almost any root vegetable, such as parsnips, turnips, carrots, and sweet potatoes.

# Mashed Root Vegetables

There are many recipes for root vegetables, but few that are as soft and soothing as this one. This is basically mashed potatoes made with other root vegetables. What isn't basic is how rich and delicious these taste.

3 red bliss potatoes or other small red-skinned potatoes

2 small carrots, cut into 2-inch pieces

1 small rutabaga, peeled and cut into 2-inch pieces

1 medium turnip, peeled and cut into 2-inch pieces

1 small parsnip, peeled and cut into 2-inch pieces

1 shallot, finely chopped

1 tablespoon kosher salt

1 teaspoon freshly ground black pepper

1 tablespoon olive oil

Warm milk (about ¼ cup)

1. In a saucepan combine the potatoes, carrots, rutabaga, turnip, parsnip, shallot, salt, and pepper. Add just enough water to come to the top of the vegetables.

2. Heat over high heat until boiling. Reduce heat to medium and simmer, covered, until much of the water has evaporated and the vegetables are all soft when tested with a fork. Drain vegetables in a colander.

3. Return empty saucepan to heat and let it get hot. Return the vegetables to the saucepan and stir them around, drying them out a bit. (They may brown a little, but that's OK.) Begin mashing the vegetables with a fork or potato masher and continue to stir around. Slowly add the olive oil. Remove from heat and mash the vegetables thoroughly with the olive oil until they are the texture of mashed potatoes. Stir in a little warm milk to make the texture smoother and softer. Keep adding warm milk until the texture is as soft as you want it. Season to taste.

Note: If you prefer, all of the vegetables can be put in a food processor and pureed. Or if you have an immersion blender, they can be pureed while still in the pot they were cooked in.

Makes: 4 to 6 servings
Nutrition Facts per serving: 173 cal., 4 g total fat (1 g sat. fat),
1 mg chol., 535 mg sodium, 32 g carbo., 5 g fiber, 4 g pro.
Daily Values: 122% vit. A, 55% vit. C, 8% calcium, 13% iron

# Smashed Potatoes with Olive Oil

A modern take on mashed potatoes, these are more rustic than refined and certainly health-conscious. We omitted the butter and cream, left on the skins, but kept the homey goodness.

1 pound red bliss potatoes or other small red-skinned potatoes, cut into 2-inch chunks

2 teaspoons kosher salt

2 tablespoons extra-virgin olive oil or canola oil

Freshly ground black pepper

1. Place the potatoes and salt in a saucepan. Add just enough water to come to the top of the potatoes. Heat over high heat until boiling. Reduce heat to medium and simmer for 10 to 15 minutes. The potatoes are done when a knife will cut through with no resistance. Drain the potatoes in a colander. Return the potatoes to the hot saucepan.

2. Smash the potatoes with a fork or with a potato masher. Stir in the oil. Season to taste with pepper.

Makes: 4 servings

Nutrition Facts per serving: 123 cal., 7 g total fat (1 g sat. fat),
0 mg chol., 246 mg sodium, 14 g carbo., 1 g fiber, 2 g pro.
Daily Values: 21% vit. C, 1% calcium, 7% iron

Vegetable Pancakes

Kids like vegetables when they're cooked well. When they're vegetable pancakes—they love them! These are crisp and golden, bursting with flavor. Bake them or sauté them in a frying pan.

1 ½ cups peeled, grated potatoes

¾ cup grated carrots

¾ cup grated zucchini

2 tablespoons grated onion

1 tablespoon chopped fresh parsley

1 teaspoon kosher salt

Freshly ground black pepper

¼ cup all-purpose flour

2 tablespoons olive oil

1. Blanch potatoes in boiling water for 1 minute. Drain in a strainer, but do not rinse. In a bowl combine the potatoes, carrots, zucchini, onion, parsley, salt, and pepper. Sprinkle flour over the vegetables and stir just until combined. Let stand for 15 to 20 minutes.

2. Shape vegetable mixture into small balls and flatten on waxed paper. Drizzle the oil in a large nonstick skillet and swirl it around until the oil coats the entire surface. Heat over medium heat until hot.

3. Transfer pancakes to skillet with a spatula. Cook about 5 minutes or until golden brown. Turn pancakes over and cook another 5 minutes. Drain on paper towels.

Note: You can also cook these pancakes in the oven. Preheat oven to 375°F. Spray a baking sheet with cooking spray. Shape vegetable mixture into small balls and flatten on the prepared baking sheet. Bake about 30 minutes or until crisp and golden brown, turning once halfway through cooking time.

Makes: 4 servings
Nutrition Facts per serving: 147 cal., 7 g total fat (1 g sat. fat), 0 mg chol., 530 mg sodium, 19 g carbo., 2 g fiber, 2 g pro.
Daily Values: 118% vit. A, 21% vit. C, 2% calcium, 6% iron

A note of reassurance from Chef Melissa: What I've learned about cooking—whether it's here at school or at home—everyone makes one bad oatmeal or inedible fish fillet. No one is perfect. Great things may come from mistakes and everyone shines in their own way.

 **Braised Collard Greens**

This goes back to my Southern heritage. For anyone south of the Mason-Dixon Line, there's nothing more familiar and satisfying than a bowl of these braised greens. Served with chicken and corn bread, it's one of my favorite meals.

2   **pounds fresh collard greens**

2   **tablespoons extra-virgin olive oil or canola oil**

1   **shallot, finely chopped**

1   **clove garlic, minced**

   Kosher salt

   Freshly ground black pepper

½   **teaspoon red wine vinegar**

1. Thoroughly wash the collard greens under cold running water. Don't shake off the water. Remove the thick, tough stems and chop the leaves into bite-size pieces.

2. Drizzle the oil in a saucepan large enough to hold all of the greens and swirl it around until the oil coats the entire surface. Heat over high heat until hot. Reduce heat to medium and add the shallot and garlic. Cook and stir until shallot is tender.

3. Add the collard greens to the saucepan and sprinkle generously with salt. Cover saucepan. After about 5 minutes, raise the lid and toss the greens around with a pair of tongs. Season with pepper. Cover and cook another 10 minutes. Remove saucepan from heat. The greens should be wilted but not soft. Sprinkle with vinegar and toss.

Makes: 4 servings

Nutrition Facts per serving: 111 cal., 7 g total fat (1 g sat. fat),
0 mg chol., 122 mg sodium, 11 g carbo., 5 g fiber, 3 g pro.
Daily Values: 232% vit. A, 97% vit. C, 29% calcium, 10% iron

 autéed Spinach with
Shallot and Crimini Mushrooms

Spinach is easy to appreciate in this tasty recipe. Sauté the shallots and mushrooms, toss in the spinach, and you're pretty much done. If you take the spinach out before it starts to wilt, it won't shrink. Three words of advice with fresh spinach: wash, wash, wash.

1	pound baby spinach
2	tablespoons olive oil
1	shallot, finely chopped
½	cup fresh crimini mushrooms, thinly sliced
¼	cup red wine vinegar
	Fine sea salt
	Freshly ground black pepper

1. Thoroughly wash spinach under cold running water. Don't shake off the water.

2. Drizzle the oil in a saucepan large enough to hold all the spinach and swirl it around until the oil coats the entire surface. Heat over high heat until hot. Reduce heat to medium and add the shallot and mushrooms. Cook and stir until the shallot is tender and mushrooms are brown.

3. Add the spinach to the saucepan. Toss the spinach around with a pair of tongs to combine the spinach with the shallots and mushrooms.

4. After cooking only 1 to 2 minutes, remove saucepan from heat. Check to see if the leaves are all wilted but not soft. Sprinkle with vinegar and toss. Season with salt and pepper.

Makes: 4 servings
Nutrition Facts per serving: 82 cal., 7 g total fat (1 g sat. fat),
0 mg chol., 236 mg sodium, 2 g carbo., 10 g fiber, 4 g pro.
Daily Values: 122% vit. A, 46% vit. C, 9% calcium, 43% iron

Braised Brussels Sprouts with Shallots

Brussels sprouts—probably the vegetable that (most unfairly, if you ask me) has the worst reputation of any other. Of course, the recipes that serve them plain and waterlogged haven't helped. Sautéed with shallots, they're delicious. The key: Don't cook them to the mushy stage; they're done when they're soft.

1	pint Brussels sprouts
2	tablespoons extra-virgin olive oil or canola oil
1	shallot, finely chopped
1	clove garlic, minced
2	tablespoons water
¼	teaspoon fresh lemon juice
	Fine sea salt
	Freshly ground black pepper

1. Trim stems and remove any wilted outer leaves from Brussels sprouts. Wash and cut Brussels sprouts in half lengthwise.

2. Drizzle the oil in a large nonstick skillet and swirl it around until the oil coats the entire surface. Heat over high heat until hot. Reduce heat to medium and add shallot and garlic. Cook and stir until tender.

3. Add Brussels sprouts to skillet and toss in the hot oil. Add water. Reduce heat to medium. Cook, covered, for 7 to 8 minutes or until sprouts are soft.

4. Remove saucepan from heat. Sprinkle sprouts with lemon juice and toss. Season to taste with salt and pepper.

Makes: 4 servings
Nutrition Facts per serving: 87 cal., 7 g total fat (1 g sat. fat),
0 mg chol., 37 mg sodium, 6 g carbo., 2 g fiber, 2 g pro.
Daily Values: 10% vit. A, 64% vit. C, 2% calcium, 4% iron

Chef Alain Sailhac, my mentor from the French Culinary Institute, once said, "Chef Bobo knows how to get kids to eat well—he knows if you push gently and nicely, you'll get them to try something." When Brussels sprouts are on the menu, we do a lot of pushing gently and nicely.

Roasted Butternut Squash

What makes this a dream recipe for the cook? You don't have to peel the squash! What makes it a dream for anyone lucky enough to eat it? The squash is so tender and sweet, it's almost like a sweet potato.

Nonstick cooking spray

1 medium butternut squash

2 tablespoons safflower or canola oil

1 teaspoon turbinado sugar or sugar

Dash ground cinnamon

1. Preheat oven to 400°F. Spray a baking sheet with cooking spray.

2. Cut the butternut squash in half lengthwise. Remove and discard all of the seeds.

3. Cut each squash half into 2-inch slices, then rub all over with the oil. Spread squash slices out on the prepared baking sheet. Combine the turbinado sugar and cinnamon, then sprinkle over the squash.

4. Roast for 15 to 20 minutes or until squash is golden brown, soft, and fragrant.

Makes: 4 servings
Nutrition Facts per serving: 128 cal., 7 g total fat (1 g sat. fat),
0 mg chol., 7 mg sodium, 16 g carbo., 3 g fiber, 2 g pro.
Daily Values: 131% vit. A, 30% vit. C, 5% calcium, 6% iron

# Roasted Zucchini
with Tomatoes and Onions

Roasted vegetables get an Italian accent with a rich harmony of flavors. The tomatoes keep the zucchini from tasting bland. This is another one of those dishes that is happy to go with just about everything.

Nonstick cooking spray

3 small zucchini

1 small red onion, thinly sliced

1 shallot, finely chopped

1 clove garlic, minced

5 sprigs fresh thyme

2 tablespoons extra-virgin olive oil or canola oil

Fine sea salt

Freshly ground black pepper

2 plum tomatoes

1. Preheat oven to 375°F. Spray a baking sheet with cooking spray.

2. Quarter zucchini lengthwise. Cut each quarter into 2- to 3-inch sticks. Put the zucchini sticks, onion, shallot, garlic, and thyme sprigs in a large bowl. Add oil and toss together. Make sure all pieces are coated with oil. Sprinkle generously with salt and pepper.

3. Cut the tomatoes in half lengthwise. Remove the core, seeds, and juice. Slice the tomatoes into very thin strips.

4. Spread the vegetables out on the prepared baking sheet. Scatter the tomato strips over the top. Roast 15 to 20 minutes or until the vegetables begin to caramelize (turn golden brown).

Makes: 4 servings
Nutrition Facts per serving: 94 cal., 7 g total fat (1 g sat. fat),
0 mg chol., 108 mg sodium, 8 g carbo., 2 g fiber, 2 g pro.
Daily Values: 14% vit. A, 31% vit. C, 3% calcium, 5% iron

Roasted Tomatoes with Garlic and Herbs

A handful of herbs, shallots, and garlic is all it takes to create a dish with intense tomato taste and a slight natural sweetness. Serve it with practically anything—I particularly like it with fish.

Nonstick cooking spray

¼ **teaspoon chopped fresh basil**

¼ **teaspoon chopped fresh thyme**

¼ **teaspoon chopped fresh oregano**

1 **shallot, finely chopped**

1 **clove garlic, minced**

6 **plum tomatoes, halved**

2 **tablespoons extra-virgin olive oil or canola oil**

Fine sea salt

Freshly ground black pepper

1. Preheat oven to 425°F. Spray a small roasting pan or baking sheet with cooking spray.

2. In a small bowl combine basil, thyme, oregano, shallot, and garlic. Put the tomatoes, cut sides up, in the prepared pan. Sprinkle a little of the herb mixture on each tomato half, then drizzle with oil.

3. Roast for 15 to 20 minutes or until the edges of the tomatoes start to turn brown. Sprinkle with salt and pepper.

Makes: 4 to 6 servings

Nutrition Facts per serving: 93 cal., 7 g total fat (1 g sat. fat),
0 mg chol., 113 mg sodium, 8 g carbo., 1 g fiber, 1 g pro.
Daily Values: 18% vit. A, 42% vit. C, 1% calcium, 4% iron

Kids love sweet tastes and vegetables are sweet. Cooked properly, especially roasted, their delicious natural sugar will come out.

 oasted Broccoli
with Pepper and Onions

Most of us don't think of including broccoli when we roast vegetables, but it's a sensational way to get all the flavor from broccoli. It turns out sweetly caramelized and still slightly crunchy.

Nonstick cooking spray

1 head broccoli

1 red bell pepper, thinly sliced

½ small red onion, thinly sliced

2 tablespoons olive oil

Kosher salt

Freshly ground black pepper

Red wine vinegar

1. Preheat oven to 350°F. Spray a baking sheet with cooking spray.

2. Cut about 1 inch off the bottom of the thick stem of the broccoli and discard. Cut the little florets of broccoli off the thick center stem. The remaining stem can be quartered lengthwise and each quarter thinly sliced.

3. Put the broccoli, bell pepper, and onion in a large bowl. Add the olive oil and toss together. Make sure all pieces are coated with oil. Sprinkle generously with salt and pepper.

4. Spread the vegetables out on the prepared baking sheet. Roast about 15 minutes or until the broccoli is fully cooked but still has a slight crunch in the bite. Transfer to a serving bowl and splash with a little vinegar.

Makes: 4 servings

Nutrition Facts per serving: 98 cal., 7 g total fat (1 g sat. fat), 0 mg chol., 97 mg sodium, 8 g carbo., 4 g fiber, 3 g pro.
Daily Values: 61% vit. A, 232% vit. C, 5% calcium, 5% iron

Steamed Broccoli

An appealing vegetable and a terrific technique: Sauteing first, then steaming the broccoli results in wonderful flavor without a hint of bitterness. Everything gets done in one pan, so the cleanup is as easy as the cooking.

1 head broccoli

1 tablespoon olive oil

1 shallot, finely chopped

¼ cup water

1 teaspoon salt

   Dash red wine vinegar

1. Cut about 1 inch off the bottom of the thick stem of the broccoli and discard. Cut the little florets of broccoli off the thick center stem. The remaining stem can be quartered lengthwise and each quarter thinly sliced.

2. Drizzle the oil in a large skillet and swirl it around until the oil coats the entire surface. Heat over high heat until hot. Reduce heat to medium and add the shallots. Cook and stir until tender.

3. Add the water and salt to skillet. Bring to boiling. Add the broccoli. Steam, covered tightly, about 7 minutes. The broccoli should be fully cooked but still firm to the bite. Sprinkle with vinegar and toss.

Makes: 4 servings

Nutrition Facts per serving: 62 cal., 4 g total fat (1 g sat. fat),
0 mg chol., 607 mg sodium, 6 g carbo., 3 g fiber, 3 g pro.
Daily Values: 28% vit. A, 118% vit. C, 5% calcium, 5% iron

S teamed Baby Bok Choy

Bok choy isn't as exotic or unusual as it sounds. Just about all of us have eaten it in Chinese food. In fact, it's sometimes called Chinese white cabbage. If you haven't cooked it before, this is a good way to start. A couple of drops of vinegar add a sprightly note to this vegetable's delicate flavor.

8   baby bok choy

1   tablespoon olive oil

1   shallot, finely chopped

¼   cup water

1   teaspoon salt

    Dash red wine vinegar

1. Very carefully trim the base of each bok choy. If you cut too much, the heads won't hold together. Remove and discard any damaged leaves.

2. Drizzle the oil in a large skillet and swirl it around until the oil coats the entire surface. Heat over high heat until hot. Reduce heat to medium and add the shallot. Cook and stir until tender.

3. Add the water and salt to skillet. Bring to boiling. Add the bok choy. Steam, covered tightly, about 3 minutes. The bok choy should be fully cooked but still have a little crunch to them. Sprinkle with vinegar and toss.

Makes: 4 servings
Nutrition Facts per serving: 59 cal., 4 g total fat (1 g sat. fat),
0 mg chol., 694 mg sodium, 5 g carbo., 2 g fiber, 3 g pro.
Daily Values: 99% vit. A, 110% vit. C, 18% calcium, 8% iron

When I started, the kids were eating one case of vegetables per day. Now that has increased to five cases per day. Because they have been introduced to boldly flavored, well-seasoned foods, their tastes have evolved, and they are willing to eat so many more fruits and vegetables.

Steamed Green Beans

Squeaky, rubbery green beans turn kids off. For perfect string beans, steam them by adding a small amount of water (only ¼ cup) to a covered skillet; don't boil them. The added shallots, olive oil, and vinegar make a great trio for maximizing flavor.

1 tablespoon olive oil

1 shallot, finely chopped

¼ cup water

1 teaspoon salt

1 pound green beans

Dash red wine vinegar

1. Drizzle the oil in a large skillet and swirl it around until the oil coats the entire surface. Heat over high heat until hot. Reduce heat to medium and add the shallot. Cook and stir until tender.

2. Add the water and salt to skillet. Bring to boiling. Add the green beans. Steam, covered tightly, about 5 minutes. The beans should be fully cooked but still have a little snap to them. Sprinkle with vinegar and toss.

Makes: 4 servings

Nutrition Facts per serving: 68 cal., 4 g total fat (0 g sat. fat),
0 mg chol., 589 mg sodium, 9 g carbo., 3 g fiber, 2 g pro.
Daily Values: 15% vit. A, 24% vit. C, 4% calcium, 7% iron

Steamed Asparagus with Shallot Dressing

A lovely spring taste that's enlivened with a Dijon mustard and lemon dressing. If you prefer, asparagus roasts beautifully as well. Top the roasted version with the same dressing.

1 **pound asparagus spears, peeled and woody stems trimmed**

¼ **cup water**

1 **shallot, finely chopped**

1 **teaspoon extra-virgin olive oil or canola oil**

1 **sprig fresh dill, finely chopped**

½ **teaspoon fresh lemon juice**

¼ **teaspoon Dijon mustard**

Fine sea salt

Freshly ground black pepper

1. Place the asparagus in a nonstick skillet. Add water. Heat over high heat until the water begins to boil. Reduce heat to low and steam, covered, until asparagus is tender, about 5 minutes.

2. For dressing, in a small bowl combine the shallot, oil, dill, lemon juice, and mustard. Stir in 1 teaspoon of the cooking liquid.

3. Place the asparagus on a serving plate. Sprinkle with salt and pepper. Drizzle dressing over asparagus.

Makes: 4 servings
Nutrition Facts per serving: 35 cal., 2 g total fat (0 g sat. fat),
0 mg chol., 118 mg sodium, 3 g carbo., 1 g fiber, 2 g pro.
Daily Values: 4% vit. A, 29% vit. C, 1% calcium, 3% iron

Yellow Squash, Mushrooms, Tomatoes, and Scallions

Here is a vegetable medley where everything is browned quickly so each vegetable holds it own. For such a simple dish, the tastes and textures are wonderfully complex.

2 tablespoons extra-virgin olive oil or canola oil

1 cup fresh button mushrooms, quartered

2 scallions, cut diagonally into small pieces

2 yellow summer squash, cut into 1-inch chunks

1 plum tomato, seeded and chopped

½ teaspoon chopped fresh thyme

Fine sea salt

Freshly ground black pepper

1. Drizzle the oil in a skillet large enough to hold all the vegetables and swirl it around until the oil coats the entire surface. Heat over high heat until hot.

2. Reduce heat to medium. Add the mushrooms and scallions to the hot skillet. Cook and stir until browned. If necessary, add a little more oil to the skillet, then add the summer squash. Toss the squash chunks around in the oil until they begin to turn golden brown.

3. When all the vegetables appear nicely browned, add the chopped tomato and thyme. Season to taste with salt and pepper.

Makes: 4 servings
Nutrition Facts per serving: 88 cal., 7 g total fat (1 g sat. fat), 0 mg chol., 106 mg sodium, 5 g carbo., 2 g fiber, 2 g pro.
Daily Values: 6% vit. A, 24% vit. C, 2% calcium, 4% iron

Because we aren't just serving "kid food," even the most finicky eaters have had their eyes opened and their palates broadened. Music to my ears? "Chef Bobo, can I have a little bit of everything?"

 **aramelized Carrots**

This is the first recipe you learn to make at cooking school—a brilliantly simple French technique of glazing carrots until they're shiny and sweet. Kids always love the sweetness!

3 medium carrots, thinly sliced
1 teaspoon butter
½ teaspoon sugar
  Water

1. Put the carrots in a nonstick skillet with the butter and sugar. Add just enough water to come halfway up on the carrots. Heat over high heat until the water begins to boil. Reduce heat to low and simmer partially covered (this steams the carrots).

2. Watch closely, and when all the water has evaporated, stir the sliced carrots around in the butter and sugar glaze left in the skillet. The carrots should look shiny and taste sweet.

Makes: 4 servings
Nutrition Facts per serving: 31 cal., 1 g total fat (1 g sat. fat),
3 mg chol., 26 mg sodium, 5 g carbo., 1 g fiber, 0 g pro.
Daily Values: 232% vit. A, 5% vit. C, 1% calcium, 1% iron

Roasted Cauliflower

I don't often say this, but here's a dish that is magic, pure and simple, all because of the cumin. Add a splash of vinegar to invigorate the cauliflower when it's done. Another bit of magic? It's probably the single most requested vegetable at Calhoun.

Nonstick cooking spray
1 head cauliflower
1 shallot, finely chopped
1 teaspoon ground cumin
2 tablespoons olive oil
Kosher salt
Freshly ground black pepper
Red wine vinegar

1. Preheat oven to 350°F. Spray a baking sheet with cooking spray.

2. Cut cauliflower into bite-size florets. Put the cauliflower and shallot in a large bowl. Sprinkle with cumin. Add the olive oil and toss together. Make sure all pieces are coated with oil. Sprinkle generously with salt and pepper.

3. Spread the vegetables out on the prepared baking sheet. Roast about 15 minutes or until the cauliflower is fully cooked but still has a slight crunch in the bite. Transfer to a serving bowl and splash with a little vinegar.

Makes: 4 servings
Nutrition Facts per serving: 95 cal., 7 g total fat (1 g sat. fat),
0 mg chol., 105 mg sodium, 7 g carbo., 3 g fiber, 2 g pro.
Daily Values: 3% vit. A, 79% vit. C, 3% calcium, 3% iron

simply sweet boy

Fruit is dessert, all by itself. Sliced ripe, sweet banana, fresh juicy raspberries, or refreshing pineapple draped with yogurt. Oh yes, there is room for the occasional scrumptious brownie or cookie...

Vanilla Butter Cookies

Here's another favorite recipe from our younger kids' cooking class. Kids really get into the "art" of baking! If you enlist help in making these cookies, be prepared for a happy kid covered with flour from head to toe.

Nonstick cooking spray

½ **cup butter, at room temperature**

½ **cup packed brown sugar**

1 **egg, beaten**

1½ **cups all-purpose flour**

1 **teaspoon pure vanilla extract**

1. Preheat oven to 350°F. Line 2 cookie sheets with parchment paper or aluminum foil, then spray the paper or foil with cooking spray.

2. Beat butter and sugar in a medium bowl with an electric mixer until light and fluffy. Beat in the egg, then add the flour and the vanilla.

3. With floured hands, divide dough into 12 equal portions and roll each portion into a ball. Place balls on prepared cookie sheets, leaving about 3 inches between cookies to allow for spreading. Press dough down slightly.

4. Bake for 12 to 15 minutes, until firm. Cool on a rack.

Orange Butter Cookies:
Prepare recipe as above, except omit the vanilla and stir in 1 teaspoon grated orange zest.

Makes: 12 cookies
Nutrition Facts per cookie: 167 cal., 9 g total fat (5 g sat. fat), 40 mg chol., 92 mg sodium, 21 g carbo., 0 g fiber, 2 g pro.
Daily Values: 7% vit. A, 2% calcium, 5% iron

What I've learned at school...

When I first started at Calhoun, my staff and I were struck by how adorable the younger kids were. The class schedule allows the second- and third-graders to eat their lunch the earliest. We looked forward to seeing these sweet faces in the lunchroom and when one of them looked up, smiled sweetly and asked for more, we'd always give it to them. How could we refuse? By the time the high school kids came into the cafeteria, we were often out of food. We realized it wasn't that the high school kids were getting too little, it was that the younger ones were getting too much. So we stopped giving them so much. Saying no to kids is hard, especially when it comes to food. You love your kids and want to feed them. But the rising obesity rate in America has a lot to do with the huge portions served. The time to start eating a sensible amount of food is when you are young.

# Honey and Oat Cookies

Just the kind of uncomplicated cookie that comes out golden, fragrant, and perfect every time. Add a glass of milk and it's comfort at its best.

Nonstick cooking spray

½ cup butter, at room temperature

¾ cup packed brown sugar

½ cup granulated sugar

2 tablespoons honey

1 egg yolk

1 cup all-purpose flour

1 cup rolled oats

½ teaspoon baking soda

¼ teaspoon salt

Dash ground cinnamon

Dash ground nutmeg

Dash ground cloves

1. Preheat oven to 375°F. Line 2 cookie sheets with parchment paper, then spray paper with cooking spray.

2. Beat butter, brown sugar, and granulated sugar in a medium bowl with an electric mixer until light and fluffy. Beat in the honey and egg yolk. Stir in flour, oats, baking soda, salt, cinnamon, nutmeg, and cloves.

3. With floured hands, divide dough into 14 equal portions and roll each portion into a ball. Place balls on prepared cookie sheets, leaving about 3 inches between cookies to allow for spreading.

4. Bake for 8 to 10 minutes or until golden and just firm. Cool on a rack.

Makes: 14 cookies
Nutrition Facts per per cookie: 201 cal., 8 g total fat (5 g sat. fat),
34 mg chol., 163 mg sodium, 32 g carbo., 1 g fiber, 2 g pro.
Daily Values: 6% vit. A, 2% calcium, 5% iron

These cookies are a foolproof favorite that little bakers love to mix with their hands!

Brownies

This recipe was the big winner with all the budding chefs in our after-school cooking program for second-, third-, and fourth-graders. The kids took their brownies home with them, and the next day I got to hear their parents rave!

Nonstick cooking spray

4 eggs

1 cup sugar

½ cup butter

1 cup chocolate chips

⅔ cup all-purpose flour

1. Preheat oven to 350°F. Spray an 8×8×2-inch baking pan with cooking spray.

2. In a large mixing bowl whisk the eggs and sugar together until combined.

3. Melt the butter in a medium saucepan. Remove from heat and stir in the chocolate chips until melted. Stir egg mixture into chocolate mixture in saucepan. Stir in flour until combined.

4. Spread brownie batter in prepared pan. Bake for 15 to 20 minutes or until brownies are cooked but still a little wobbly (not set in the center). Cool in pan on a rack.

Makes: 12 brownies

Nutrition Facts per brownie: 249 cal., 14 g total fat (8 g sat. fat),
92 mg chol., 101 mg sodium, 31 g carbo., 1 g fiber, 3 g pro.
Daily Values: 8% vit. A, 2% calcium, 6% iron

Flourless Chocolate Cake

After we developed this rich bittersweet chocolate cake, we made it with the high school Cooking Club one afternoon before winter break. They loved it so much that when they came back from the holidays, all but one of them had baked the cake at home to their families' delight!

6 ounces bittersweet chocolate

6 tablespoons butter or soy margarine

¼ cup cocoa powder

4 egg whites

Pinch cream of tartar

¼ cup sugar

1 recipe Coconut Sorbet (optional)

Coconut Sorbet:
In a saucepan make a syrup by combining ½ cup less 2 tablespoons of sugar and ¼ cup water. Cook and stir until sugar is dissolved; let cool. Stir syrup into 1 can of unsweetened coconut milk; process in ice cream machine according to the manufacturer's directions.

Makes: 1 pint.
Nutrition Facts per ½ cup: 239 cal., 17 g total fat, (15 g sat. fat), 0 mg chol., 24 mg sodium, 21 g carb., 0 g fiber, 2 g pro.
Daily Values: 5% iron

1. Preheat oven to 400°F. Coat the insides of six 2½-inch muffin cups generously with butter and dust with sugar. Store in the freezer until ready to use.

2. Melt chocolate and butter in double boiler; remove from heat. Stir in cocoa powder and let cool.

3. In a large mixing bowl whisk egg whites and cream of tartar until foamy. Sift in the sugar; beat to soft meringue stage. The egg whites will hold peaks when you lift a little from the bowl with a whisk. Be very careful not to overbeat the egg whites because they will become watery.

4. Gradually fold ¼ of the beaten egg whites into the chocolate mixture. Be very delicate in this step so as not to lose the air whipped into the egg whites. When well combined, fold in the remainder of the egg whites until blended. The mixture doesn't have to be perfectly combined—if your batter has a marbled appearance, it works just fine.

5. Remove the prepared muffin cups from the freezer and spoon in the chocolate and egg white mixture until filled just below the top of the cup.

6. Bake for 7 to 8 minutes until outside is set but inside is still gooey. The cakes will rise above the edge of the cup. Remove from oven; let rest 3 minutes before inverting. Use an offset spatula to transfer the cakes to a plate; serve with the Coconut Sorbet, if you like.

Makes: 6 servings
Nutrition Facts per serving without Coconut Sorbet: 399 cal., 33 g total fat (20 g sat. fat), 62 mg chol., 273 mg sodium, 26 g carbo., 2 g fiber, 5 g pro.
Daily Values: 18% vit. A, 6% calcium, 8% iron

Coconut Macaroons

These light, delicate macaroons are simple to prepare. Kids love lining up the small spoonfuls on cookie sheets. Set a plate of them on the table when you're serving a fruit dessert or ice cream and watch them disappear!

3 egg whites

¼ teaspoon pure vanilla extract

5⅓ cups sweetened flaked coconut

½ cup sugar

1. Preheat oven to 300°F. Line 2 cookie sheets with parchment paper.

2. In a large mixing bowl beat the egg whites and vanilla with an electric mixer until stiff. Stir together the coconut and sugar; fold into beaten egg whites with a large rubber scraper.

3. Drop by spoonfuls, about 1 inch in diameter, onto prepared cookie sheets, leaving about 1 inch between cookies to allow for spreading. Bake macaroons for 15 minutes. Cool on a rack.

Makes: 45 to 60 cookies
Nutrition Facts per per cookie: 76 cal., 5 g total fat (5 g sat. fat),
0 mg chol., 46 mg sodium, 8 g carbo., 1 g fiber, 1 g pro.

I am a believer in the occasional scrumptious brownie or cookie, but the majority of dessert we serve is fresh fruit.

# Maple Vanilla Granola

This granola has more flavor and freshness than anything you could buy in a store and it's so easy to make. The vanilla brings out all the taste of the maple. Add raisins, dried cranberries, or nuts after it's cooked, if you like. Serve this crunchy treat as a breakfast cereal or dessert topped with vanilla yogurt and fresh fruit.

Nonstick cooking spray

5 cups old-fashioned rolled oats

½ cup packed brown sugar

1 teaspoon salt

½ teaspoon ground cinnamon

⅓ cup vegetable oil

¼ cup pure maple syrup

¼ cup honey

1 tablespoon pure vanilla extract

1. Preheat oven to 300°F. Line a large baking sheet with parchment paper or aluminum foil, then spray paper or foil with cooking spray.

2. In a large bowl mix the oats, brown sugar, salt, and cinnamon until combined.

3. In another bowl mix the oil, maple syrup, honey, and vanilla. Pour the honey mixture over the oat mixture and mix together with your hands. (Plastic gloves are a must for this!)

4. Spread granola on prepared baking sheet. Bake about 30 minutes or until golden brown. Cool and store in an airtight container.

Makes: 16 servings

Nutrition Facts per ½ cup serving: 217 cal., 7 g total fat (1 g sat. fat), 0 mg chol., 150 mg sodium, 36 g carbo., 3 g fiber, 4 g pro.
Daily Values: 3% calcium, 8% iron

Orange Sections, Mint Leaves, and Honey

An inspired idea for a fresh fruit dessert—just adding mint and honey makes the flavors sing. If you need to convince someone how truly wonderful fresh fruit can be, set a serving of this delightful dish in front of him or her.

4   navel oranges

¼   cup fresh mint leaves

2   tablespoons honey

1   recipe Vanilla Yogurt Cheese (page 217) (optional)

1. Prepare the oranges by peeling them and then cutting into sections. Place orange sections in a bowl and stir in the mint leaves. Drizzle with honey. Serve with Vanilla Yogurt Cheese, if you like. Serve immediately.

Makes: 4 servings

Nutrition Facts per serving: 61 cal., 0 g total fat (0 g sat. fat), 0 mg chol., 1 mg sodium, 16 g carbo., 1 g fiber, 1 g pro.

Daily Values: 2% vit. A, 59% vit. C, 3% calcium, 6% iron

F resh Pineapple and Honey

We discovered this easy recipe one year when the students were focusing on the culture of Tanzania for Calhoun's annual Harvest Festival. We researched traditional Tanzanian recipes and found this one to be sweet, refreshing, healthful, and delicious. It's a great example of how sensational something simple can be.

1 fresh pineapple
Nonstick cooking spray
½ cup honey
Vanilla yogurt

1. Cut the top and the bottom off the pineapple. Peel the pineapple by cutting down the sides in long strokes. Make sure you cut out the little "eyes" that may be left along the sides after you have removed the outside skin. Cut the pineapple into chunks or slices.

2. Spray a large skillet with cooking spray. Heat over high heat until hot. Add the pineapple chunks and cook and stir until they begin to caramelize and turn brown. Remove from heat and drizzle with honey. Serve immediately with vanilla yogurt.

3. Or if you are cooking outdoors, grill the pineapple slices. Spray the pineapple on both sides with cooking spray and place on a hot grill. After a couple of minutes on one side, flip them over and let the other side cook for a couple of minutes. When nicely browned, remove the slices from the grill and drizzle with honey. Serve immediately with vanilla yogurt.

Makes: 6 servings
Nutrition Facts per serving: 123 cal., 0 g total fat (0 g sat. fat),
0 mg chol., 2 mg sodium, 33 g carbo., 1 g fiber, 0 g pro.
Daily Values: 20% vit. C, 1% calcium, 2% iron

The smaller children eat lunch in their classrooms, and they must be seated before we serve dessert. At the mere mention of "dessert," they scatter like mice and run for their chairs. It's incredible!

# **M**ixed Berries, Apples, and Bananas

So versatile, this lightly sugared fruit mixture is a perfect after-school snack or a real treat spooned over French toast for breakfast. Or go all out and spoon it over Vanilla Yogurt Cheese (page 217), then sprinkle with Maple Vanilla Granola (page 212).

I Gala or Fuji apple,
  peeled, cored, and cut
  into small chunks

I banana, peeled and cut into
  small chunks

I teaspoon fresh lemon juice

I cup strawberries, stemmed
  and halved

I cup blueberries

I cup raspberries

I tablespoon sugar

I. In a large bowl combine the apple and banana. Sprinkle with the lemon juice and toss. (The lemon juice will keep the apples and bananas from oxidizing and turning brown.)

2. Stir in the strawberries, blueberries, and raspberries. Sprinkle with the sugar and toss. Cover and chill about I hour before serving.

Makes: 6 servings
Nutrition Facts per serving: 69 cal., 0 g total fat (0 g sat. fat),
0 mg chol., 2 mg sodium, 17 g carbo., 3 g fiber, I g pro.
Daily Values: 2% vit. A, 41% vit. C, I% calcium, 2% iron

Vanilla Yogurt Cheese

This is simply low-fat vanilla yogurt with most of the water drained out of it. In addition to being healthful, it's fun for kids to make. It makes a creamy, luxurious-textured puddinglike dessert. Top it with fresh fruit and/or granola. A little drizzle of honey is good, too, and harks back to its Greek origins.

Cotton cheesecloth or a white cotton napkin

1 **quart low-fat vanilla yogurt**

Butcher twine

1. Line a colander with a double thickness of cheesecloth or a white cotton napkin.

2. Spoon all the yogurt into the center of the cloth. (Wash and save the yogurt container to use later.) Bring up the sides of the cheesecloth all the way around so that the yogurt is literally encased in a bag.

3. Use the butcher twine to tie the gathered sides together. Wrap the twine around the bottom 2 or 3 times in different directions to hold the yogurt stable.

4. Hang the bag of yogurt over a sink or bowl and let its water drip out for up to 12 hours. (The longer it drips, the thicker the texture of the cheese.)

5. Discard the water and unwrap the cheese. It will be thick and look like a ball of cream cheese.

6. Put the cheese in a wire strainer and push it through the strainer with a spoon. This makes the texture of the cheese smooth and velvety.

7. Put the yogurt cheese back into the original container. Chill until ready to use.

Makes: 8 servings
Nutrition Facts per ¼-cup serving: 104 cal., 2 g total fat (1 g sat. fat),
6 mg chol., 81 mg sodium, 17 g carbo., 0 g fiber, 6 g pro.
Daily Values: 1% vit. A, 2% vit. C, 21% calcium

Banana Sorbet

Three ingredients and three simple steps almost magically transform ripe bananas into an icy after-dinner treat your whole family will love. It doesn't get better than this!

4 ripe bananas, frozen

1 tablespoon honey

1 teaspoon fresh lime juice

Honey, chocolate sauce, and/or chopped nuts (optional)

1. Peel the frozen bananas, then cut them into 1-inch chunks. Put the bananas, honey, and lime juice in a food processor. Process until pureed. Transfer to a freezer container. Cover and freeze.

2. To serve, scoop into individual serving dishes. Drizzle with additional honey or chocolate sauce and sprinkle with nuts, if you like.

Note: If you like, put a little Vanilla Yogurt Cheese (page 217) in the processor with the bananas for an even creamier dessert!

Makes: 4 to 6 servings
Nutrition Facts per serving: 83 cal., 0 g total fat (0 g sat. fat),
0 mg chol., 1 mg sodium, 21 g carbo., 2 g fiber, 1 g pro.
Daily Values: 1% vit. A, 12% vit. C, 1% calcium, 1% iron

I firmly believe that fruit is dessert, but that doesn't mean it has to be plain and boring. This sorbet is the perfect case in point. Because the bananas are naturally sweet, you only need to add a little bit of honey to make it just right.

index

Numbers in orange indicate photo.

index

Numbers in orange indicate photo.

metric information

The charts on this page provide a guide for converting measurements from the U.S. customary system, which is used throughout this book, to the metric system.

Product Differences

Most of the ingredients called for in the recipes in this book are available in most countries. However, some are known by different names. Here are some common American ingredients and their possible counterparts:

- Sugar (white) is granulated, fine granulated, or castor sugar.
- Powdered sugar is icing sugar.
- All-purpose flour is enriched, bleached or unbleached white household flour. When self-rising flour is used in place of all-purpose flour in a recipe that calls for leavening, omit the leavening agent (baking soda or baking powder) and salt.
- Light-colored corn syrup is golden syrup.
- Cornstarch is cornflour.
- Baking soda is bicarbonate of soda.
- Vanilla or vanilla extract is vanilla essence.
- Green, red, or yellow sweet peppers are capsicums or bell peppers.
- Golden raisins are sultanas.

Volume and Weight

The United States traditionally uses cup measures for liquid and solid ingredients. The chart below shows the approximate imperial and metric equivalents. If you are accustomed to weighing solid ingredients, the following approximate equivalents will be helpful.

- 1 cup butter, castor sugar, or rice = 8 ounces = ½ pound = 250 grams
- 1 cup flour = 4 ounces = ¼ pound = 125 grams
- 1 cup icing sugar = 5 ounces = 150 grams
- Canadian and U.S. volume for a cup measure is 8 fluid ounces (237 ml), but the standard metric equivalent is 250 ml.
- 1 British imperial cup is 10 fluid ounces.
- In Australia, 1 tablespoon equals 20 ml, and there are 4 teaspoons in the Australian tablespoon.

Spoon measures are used for smaller amounts of ingredients. Although the size of the tablespoon varies slightly in different countries, for practical purposes and for recipes in this book, a straight substitution is all that's necessary. Measurements made using cups or spoons always should be level unless stated otherwise.

Common Weight Range Replacements

Imperial / U.S.	Metric
½ ounce	15 g
1 ounce	25 g or 30 g
4 ounces (¼ pound)	115 g or 125 g
8 ounces (½ pound)	225 g or 250 g
16 ounces (1 pound)	450 g or 500 g
1¼ pounds	625 g
1½ pounds	750 g
2 pounds or 2¼ pounds	1,000 g or 1 Kg

Oven Temperature Equivalents

Fahrenheit Setting	Celsius Setting*	Gas Setting
300°F	150°C	Gas Mark 2 (very low)
325°F	160°C	Gas Mark 3 (low)
350°F	180°C	Gas Mark 4 (moderate)
375°F	190°C	Gas Mark 5 (moderate)
400°F	200°C	Gas Mark 6 (hot)
425°F	220°C	Gas Mark 7 (hot)
450°F	230°C	Gas Mark 8 (very hot)
475°F	240°C	Gas Mark 9 (very hot)
500°F	260°C	Gas Mark 10 (extremely hot)
Broil	Broil	Grill

*Electric and gas ovens may be calibrated using celsius. However, for an electric oven, increase celsius setting 10 to 20 degrees when cooking above 160°C. For convection or forced air ovens (gas or electric) lower the temperature setting 25°F/10°C when cooking at all heat levels.

Baking Pan Sizes

Imperial / U.S.	Metric
9x1½-inch round cake pan	22- or 23x4-cm (1.5 L)
9x1½-inch pie plate	22- or 23x4-cm (1 L)
8x8x2-inch square cake pan	20x5-cm (2 L)
9x9x2-inch square cake pan	22- or 23x4.5-cm (2.5 L)
11x7x1½-inch baking pan	28x17x4-cm (2 L)
2-quart rectangular baking pan	30x19x4.5-cm (3 L)
13x9x2-inch baking pan	34x22x4.5-cm (3.5 L)
15x10x1-inch jelly roll pan	40x25x2-cm
9x5x3-inch loaf pan	23x13x8-cm (2 L)
2-quart casserole	2 L

U.S. / Standard Metric Equivalents

⅛ teaspoon = 0.5 ml	
¼ teaspoon = 1 ml	
½ teaspoon = 2 ml	
1 teaspoon = 5 ml	
1 tablespoon = 15 ml	
2 tablespoons = 25 ml	
¼ cup = 2 fluid ounces = 50 ml	
⅓ cup = 3 fluid ounces = 75 ml	
½ cup = 4 fluid ounces = 125 ml	
⅔ cup = 5 fluid ounces = 150 ml	
¾ cup = 6 fluid ounces = 175 ml	
1 cup = 8 fluid ounces = 250 ml	
2 cups = 1 pint = 500 ml	
1 quart = 1 litre	

Thank you ❤ Chef Bobo Kelsey
Tons for ♡
your excellent I Love your
food. And food. you Make ♡
hard work. the school special

Thank you for being Love Hadley ☺
chefs

Your Food is the

The food this year.
great this year.
I love your food
that you make.
too love Jamica

Best!!

Dear
bobo
Thank you
for the
good food
this year!
Maggie

Thank you for cooking for us ♥ a hole ♥ yeah Jessica ♥

Dear Baba, your food was good. Zachary

You make fabulous deserts! —Tommy—

I did not like your food I Loved it so thanks you Love Lily

i love your pizza from NICO

I likt the foods bat. Samfods.

Shef Bo B and I will love osher

P.S. I Ka-C

the pizza and hamburgers are great Jack

Your food is the best. Ryan

Thank You Cheyenne ♥

Lu